Date Due

MAY 2 8 1990			

DA CAPO PRESS SERIES IN
ARCHITECTURE AND DECORATIVE ART
General Editor: ADOLF K. PLACZEK
Avery Librarian, Columbia University

VOLUME 4

Gravestones
Of Early New England

GRAVESTONES
Of Early New England

And the Men Who Made Them

1653 – 1800

by
Harriette Merrifield Forbes

DA CAPO PRESS • NEW YORK • 1967

*An unabridged republication of the first edition
published by Houghton Mifflin Company in 1927 in Boston,
this Da Capo Press edition is published by special arrangement
with Houghton Mifflin Company.*

*Da Capo Press is grateful to
the American Antiquarian Society, Worcester, Massachusetts,
for making available the original negatives for the illustrations.*

Library of Congress Catalog Card Number 67-27452

*© 1967 Da Capo Press
A Division of Plenum Publishing Corporation
227 West 17 Street, New York, N. Y. 10011*

Printed in the United States of America

GRAVESTONES
of *Early New England*
And the Men who Made Them

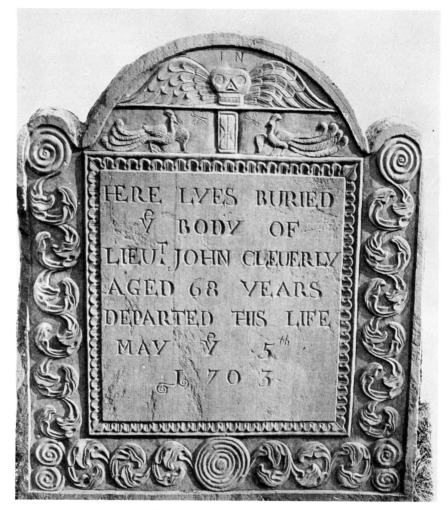

JOHN CLEVERLY, QUINCY, 1703

GRAVESTONES

of *Early New England*

And the Men who made them
1653–1800

By
Harriette Merrifield Forbes

With illustrations from Photographs by the Author

BOSTON
Printed by *The Riverside Press* for HOUGHTON MIFFLIN
COMPANY in PARK STREET near the COMMON
MDCCCCXXVII

To
My Family
who for several years
have turned aside from their own interests
to wander with me in the
old burying-grounds
of
New England

PREFACE

IT would not be possible in a book of this size to cover adequately the subject of early New England Gravestones. I have tried to select for reproduction some of the most noteworthy, and others not so noteworthy but interesting because their maker is a matter of record. A few stonecutters who seemed to be the most popular in their own generation have been chosen as a type of them all. There were many others; some who did equally good work.

The greater part of the book is devoted to the gravestones in and around Boston, and the towns mentioned by name are all in Massachusetts, unless otherwise stated.

I am most indebted to the American Antiquarian Society for the constant use of their valuable library. I wish to thank also the Worcester Art Museum, the Massachusetts Historical Society, the New England Historic Genealogical Society, and the many friends who have given me help and encouragement.

HARRIETTE MERRIFIELD FORBES

WORCESTER

CONTENTS

GRAVESTONES
of *Early New England*
∵

CHAPTER I

THE SPIRIT OF THE GRAVESTONE

THE spirit of our New England forefathers speaks from their
gravestones:

> 'Keep death and judgment always in your eye,
> None's fit to live but who is fit to die.'

Up to the middle of the eighteenth century death was a diversion
in their monotonous lives. A great funeral was a great spectacle for
the populace. There were no circuses to come to town. There was
no Christmas, no May Day, no Fourth of July. A good funeral was
appreciated by every one, especially if the wealth and importance of
the deceased justified not only black housings and black stockings
upon the horses, but death's heads upon their foreheads and glitter-
ing armorial escutcheons upon their flanks.

We find record after record of general extravagance. For instance,
when Waitstill Winthrop died, nearly twenty-two pounds — a pro-
digious sum — was paid for painting hatchments, silk and buckram
escutcheons, large and small crests, and 'foreheads' for the horses.
Sometimes our thrifty ancestors used these coats-of-arms and dark
trappings to decorate their homes and pulpits. All might gaze upon
these symbols of this world's pomp, and consider the words of the
preacher who taught that 'all is vanity' and thus be better prepared
for the future.

The artistic handicraft men had more orders on the occasion of a
rich man's death, than ever his life afforded. Death was the source of
their richest rewards and greatest inspiration. The deathly trappings
of the funeral horses, the pallbearers' embroidered gloves, the
mourners'

mourners' rings, the escutcheons now are gone. The gravestones alone remain. To our day they stand, shoulder to shoulder, in hundreds of New England graveyards, the one unchanging record of the Puritan's reverence for death, and appropriately enough, the most lavish and original of all their artistic endeavors. The colonists used their finest skill and raised their most enduring and characteristic works of art in *memento mori*.

They are the only things now remaining which the men and women of two hundred and more years ago would recognize should they be able to come back to the places that once knew them. How bewildered and lonely Judge Sewall would be in the streets where he once walked, until he found himself in King's Chapel, Copp's Hill, or the Granary and caught sight of the old table tombs where he once sat and the upright gravestones with the very same inscriptions he used to read.

Everything that they made, their houses, churches, pewter, table ware, furniture, is 'seemly' and often beautiful. But upon the furniture, the silver or brass, they lavished no such originality or creative force of decoration. Not even in the early paintings is expressed any conscious philosophy or attitude towards life. In the carvings of the gravestones, often very beautiful, always thoughtful, we meet the most characteristic expression of the Puritan as artist. What the totem pole was to the Alaskan Indians was the gravestone to the first six generations of New-Englanders. It seems to me there can be no serious consideration of him as artist or thinker without some study in this field. We have little other sculpture from his austere hand, and yet upon the graves — as I try to show by my photographs — are many admirable contemporary portraits, arrangements of flowers and fruits almost renaissant in their richness and beauty; there are ships cut in stone with the rigging of the day; even God himself is pictured rolling up the firmament, in Newport, Rhode Island, and also in Rhode Island one may see Adam and Eve stand naked and ashamed. Incidentally the lettering used is often of extraordinary purity and charm of proportion.

To-day there is none of the harshness and starkness of death in the old burying-grounds of old New England. Perhaps because the

Puritan

HEAR SLEAPS THAT
BLESED ON—WHOES LIEF
GOD HELP VS ALL TO LIVE
THAT SO WHEN TIEM SHALLBE
THAT WE THIS WORLD MVST LEVE
WE EVER MAY BE HAPPY
WITH BLESED WILLIAM PADDY

WILLIAM PADDY, KING'S CHAPEL, 1658

Near Here Lyes The Body of
Mr William Wells The Oldest
Son of William Wells Esqr
Who Departed This Life In
October 1696 Aged About
37 Years

WILLIAM WELLS, SOUTHOLD, L. I., 1696

SARAH PRESCOTT, LANCASTER, 1709

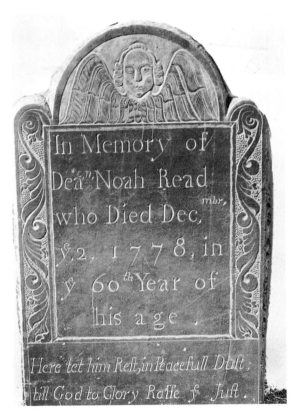

NOAH READ, ATTLEBOROUGH, 1778

Puritan lived so in the presence of the Black Angel, he came to have little fear of him. With Saint Francis, he might have addressed him as 'my brother — the death of the body.' The French, so often called a gay people, make their cemeteries morbid and repellent to the living, but the grave and other-worldly Puritan accepted death with such passionate faith in a better world to come that we may believe that his fears were quieted. His sunny hillside burying-grounds with their carved stones remain to this day peaceful and blessed spots.

I wish that it were possible for us to look at these old stones with the eyes of the seventeenth and eighteenth centuries. Then we should not smile at the spelling nor find either epitaph or ornamentation 'quaint' or amusing. Then should we be warned by their warnings, comforted by their consolations. It was for this purpose that they stand — to point a moral as well as to adorn a grave. They honored the dead and they taught the living. The ministers and the learned men of the day loved to write epitaphs. Cotton Mather, who more than any other man of his time controlled the thought of the people, did not consider the obituary of a friend complete unless he had added an 'epitaphium' in rhyme, sometimes in Latin, sometimes in English. Few, only the ministers and the rare college graduates, could read the Latin upon the stones. Many could not even read the English, but all, even the most ignorant, could see the carving and understand the message thus made visual.

The graves of old England clustered around the church in the churchyard. In New England, there was neither church nor churchyard in the earliest days, but meeting-house and burying-ground. In the meeting-houses, Mr. Mather and his fellow ministers told their congregations where in the Bible could be found the story of the 'great stone of Abel' erected by his father Adam, with the inscription, 'Here was shed the blood of the righteous Abel' — the very first gravestone mentioned in the history of the world; and the eyes of the people turned to the sunny burying-ground just outside the windows and the stones they had placed in memory of their children and friends.

To-day you may ride through New England by-ways and see beyond the crumbling stone walls, gay with ivy and woodbine, close

to

to where once stood a tiny meeting-house, the great owl eyes of the grinning death's heads. You may almost hear the beat of those scaly carved stone wings; almost hear those ghostly voices: 'As I am now, so you must be . .' or '*memento mori.*'

In old Bennington, Vermont, who can forget those white marble monuments, festive with grapes and staring angels, or that persistent cry, seemingly wrung from a human soul, 'O Relentless Death'? Pause for a moment in any of these old burying-grounds. Walk about you. It will be well worth your time, and when you drive on it will be with greater understanding and I think reverence for the past. You will be conscious of that courageous and indomitable spirit of our Puritan ancestors which would not fear even Death.

CHAPTER II
THE SUBSTANCE OF THE GRAVESTONE

ALTHOUGH designed to appeal to man's spiritual nature, the gravestone was a thing of substance. It had to be made by some one — out of such materials as he found fitting and available. Some one, too, had to select a proper form of ornamentation for it, and when it was quite ready for the market it had to be sold to one desiring it. We must delve in the dusty records of the past to discover if we can some suggestions about how this business of the gravestone was conducted. Perhaps the stones themselves may prove to be less mute and impassive than they seem. They spoke to their own generation of the certainty and glory of a future life, to ours they may reveal something of the life this earlier generation lived.

We may divide our research into five distinct topics:

I. Were the gravestones imported as such from England or other foreign country?

II. Were the stones from which they were made imported? If not, where was the material procured?

III. How were they bought and sold?

IV. What kind of men made them?

V. Where did the makers of them get their designs?

I. WERE THE EARLY GRAVESTONES IMPORTED?

Were these early stones imported, either carved and ready for an inscription or carved and lettered and ready to be 'set' by some local man? Or were they the product of the craftsmen of the New World?

The statement that they were imported has been made so many times that it would seem as if there must be some basis for it. Not long ago, when I was wandering in an old burying-ground near Boston and looking at a stone made about 1775, a window in a neighboring house was opened, and a woman's voice called out to know why I was interested in that stone. 'It was imported from England,'

England,' she said; 'they were all imported from England. My mother always told me so.' And yet her grandmother was probably a contemporary of Thomas Park, who made it, and the slate of which it was made was quarried in Harvard. She would not have believed me had I told her. Undoubtedly some stones were imported. It would seem a natural thing to do. The question is, Did they to any great extent bring over from England or elsewhere gravestones which had been carved abroad? In other words, were there men in New England of sufficient artistic and technical skill to make the many fine ones which are still in existence?

I. First, we can say very definitely that there were skilled workmen in New England. Writing about 1697, Cotton Mather says that in the twelve years succeeding the granting of a charter to the Massachusetts Bay Company in 1628/29, 'artificers to the number of some thousands' were moved 'to transplant themselves and their families into New England.' In 1676, Edward Randolph wrote to the Privy Council in London about conditions as he was finding them in Boston, and he says, 'There are rich men of all callings and professions and all mechanical arts and occupations thrive well.'

A year later there was a petition presented to the General Court by one hundred and twenty-nine 'Handycraftsmen, a very considerable part of the Town of Boston,' praying for protection in their several callings.

II. If imported to any great extent, we should expect to find them listed in the ladings of the ships of that period. I have examined hundreds of such bills and have found in them nearly all the necessities and luxuries of life, but no mention of gravestones. The theory is that they were brought in as ballast, but grindstones, which would make equally good ballast, appear on many of the lists.

III. There are many letters still in existence ordering from England every variety of article for the convenience and use of the New-Englanders. But with one or two late exceptions no gravestones are so ordered.

IV. If imported, they would naturally be handled by the merchants. The inventories of the day were exceedingly full, a cracked cup or half a yard of ribbon never escaping the lynx eyes of the 'prizer.'

PRUDENCE WHITWELL, MARBLEHEAD, 1773

ELIZABETH GREENLEAF, NEWBURY, 1712

THOMAS BANCROFT, WAKEFIELD, 1691

JOSEPH LARNED, PUTNAM, CONN., 1756

'prizer.' Surely if the merchants of the day had gravestones among their wares, they would have been mentioned in these very long lists. I have found no allusion to them in the many which I have examined. The nearest approach is in that of the merchant, John Winslow, taken in 1683, where one of the items is slate in the yard 17/ and among the debts owing from the estate 'To Nathaniel Peirce for ye slate £17.00.' This may have been Nathaniel Pierce, who was a sea captain, and the slate may have been imported, but slate is not gravestones and was used for many other purposes.

Again, if handled by the merchants, it would have been merchants who were paid for them. I have found no case where a merchant was paid before 1743, when Mary Shore died and William Parkman rendered an account for 'gloves, gravestones &c.' That same year his daughter had married Joshua Emmes, a maker of gravestones, which makes it easy to guess that William Parkman was helping his new son-in-law.

We can safely say that the merchants neither bought nor sold gravestones except under some unusual circumstances; a fact which seems to be almost conclusive proof that it was a local business carried on in this country by the stonecutters themselves, in such a way that the vast majority of the people were satisfied.

II. MATERIALS

The slates and clay stones, greenstones, schists, and freestones from which the early gravestones are made are quite bewildering to the ordinary individual. The first question we naturally ask is whether all these different materials were found here ready at hand, or whether they were brought over from England or elsewhere.

I do not know that the Reverend Cotton Mather was trying to state an historical fact, when, in speaking of the highly complimentary epitaph of the Reverend Urian Oakes in 1693, he writes, 'And know, reader, that though the stones in this wilderness are already grown so witty as to speak, they never yet that I could hear of, grew so wicked as to lye.'

But undoubtedly many of the earliest gravestones were made from the stones of the wilderness. The geologists tell us that the thick
solid

solid blocks of 'greenstone' which we find in the old burying-grounds, like that placed to the memory of William Paddy, King's Chapel, 1658, were without much doubt shaped from the boulders of Boston and vicinity.

In fact, in every old burying-ground, we find the field stones of the country used for gravestones; sometimes the lettering on them is good, at other times exceedingly poor. In many of these cases it was not a skilled stonecutter who did the work — more likely some friend of the deceased. An early and rather pathetic example of these home-made stones is that of Sarah Prescott, Lancaster, quite unshaped, and lettered by one whose knowledge of spelling and stonecutting was about equal. We can imagine how laboriously he toiled to make it known that Sarah's 'blased soul' 'asanded up to Heaven July 14 1709.' These field stones are naturally of every sort and variety.

It is a much more difficult and interesting problem when we study the slates, which, even when only lettered, usually show a skilled hand.

It seems to be a well-grounded tradition that many of the early slate stones were imported, and this probably accounts for the rather widespread belief that the carved stones came also from England and Wales.

There was no need to import slate. As early as 1630, the Reverend Francis Higginson, writing a description of the New England of that early time, says, 'For stone there is plenty of slate at the Isle of Slate in Massachusetts Bay.' Slate Island, like the other islands in the Bay, was appropriated by the General Court 'to publique benefit and uses and to remain in the power of the Govr. and Assistants (for the time being) to be lett and disposed of by them to help towards publique charges.' And we find in 1633 and again in 1650 that Slate Island was so let, but with the condition that 'it shall be free for any man to make use of the slate.'

There were, however, many uses for slate besides making gravestones, and whether the slate of Slate Island was ever used for this latter purpose is not known.

Professor Woodworth, of Harvard, in an article read before the Cambridge

ANN ERINTON, CAMBRIDGE, 1653

PHINEHAS PRATT, CHARLESTOWN, 1680

ANNA CUTLER, CHARLESTOWN, 1683

THOMAS RAND, CHARLESTOWN, 1683

Cambridge Historical Society on 'The Origin of the Old Burial Yard Stones,' tells us that many of the Cambridge gravestones resemble the local varieties of the argillites of Somerville. He finds others of light-colored slate crossed by whitish bands of a sandy texture which are like rocks cropping out near Squantum. He thinks, however, that the quarries at Squantum were not worked until about 1724 — they furnished the so-called Braintree slate from which many of the old gravestones were said to have been made. There was also an early quarry in Cambridge.

Professor Wolff says that we can distinguish Welsh slate by the bands of various colors crossing its surface.

It was not uncommon for a stonecutter to be also a mariner, or at least to have a brother or other relative who was, and it would be extremely easy to bring over a load of English or Welsh slate, and this may have been done in the earliest days. Later we find all kinds of slate used, usually the gravestones in any particular locality being obtained from some near-by quarry. In fact the presence of such a quarry attracted stonecutters to that vicinity, which accounts partly at least for the groups we find working together.

For instance, in what the geologists call the Narragansett Basin between Providence, Rhode Island, and Wrentham, Massachusetts, there are beds of shaly slates, many of them showing quite delightful coloring in shades of rose and green. In North Attleborough there is a vein of rock, in a soft olive green, with layers of dull red, and many a gravestone was cut with one color on the surface, the other for the background, making a very charming cameo. Other stones in the burying-grounds in this vicinity show other very interesting combinations of color. In Attleborough that of Deacon Noah Read, 1778, is a deep orange with letters and background in a clear cobalt.

Another interesting cameo is gray with the design in a dull orange, and more common are gray and blue or gray and black — the black usually being used for the design and gray for the background. We find these cameos most abundant in the vicinity of Wrentham, although occasionally they seem to have been sent to quite distant places. In Wrentham there are very early irregular stones, roughly
lettered

lettered of the seventeenth or early eighteenth century, but instead of the usual gray of our field stones, they are of a soft rose color, apparently unfaded after their two hundred years of exposure to sun and storm.

What more charming material could a stonecutter choose than the colored shaly slates of the Narragansett Basin? Many a sculptor thought so, and there was an interesting succession of local men working in Attleborough, Wrentham, Bellingham, and other towns in that vicinity.

Cameo stones were also made from a kind of quartzite with layers of black hornblende. Quartzite in combination with other substances was used almost exclusively by a man or group of men working in Belchertown and vicinity from the middle of the eighteenth until well into the nineteenth century. Most of their stones are a plain gray, but occasionally there is one of a translucent white, a very charming material for this purpose. Sometimes gayer colors take the place of the black, gray, and white. In the old burying-ground at Warren, Massachusetts, there are some very interesting color effects, soft shades of red and yellow and purple predominating over the 'sad' colors, thus making the sunny hillside a cheerful spot.

In Plymouth County they were not so fortunate. Hundreds of gravestones are made from a green schist which cracks and splits, and before many more years will cease to be.

Later the quarries of Harvard and Lancaster, many in Vermont, some in Rhode Island and Connecticut, furnished all the slate necessary for gravestones and probably very little was imported after the early years of the eighteenth century.

From almost the earliest times the red and brown sandstones of Connecticut were quarried and used for gravestones. In Windsor, Connecticut, was the 'Hayden Stone Pit' worked by William Hayden as early as 1654 and perhaps earlier, as we are told that the gravestone of the Reverend Ephraim Huit, who died in 1644, was taken from it and is still standing in the Windsor burying-ground. The writer of the 'Hayden Genealogy' was born in 1811 and he says an old man many years ago told him that it was ever the practice, when quarrying at the old stone pit, 'to reserve the slabs which were

suitable

NEAL CHILDREN, GRANARY, 1671

CUTLER CHILDREN, CHARLESTOWN, 1680

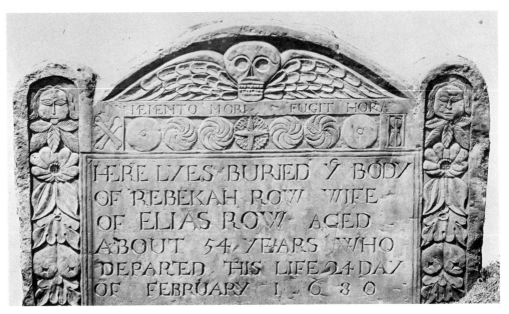

REBEKAH ROW, CHARLESTOWN, 1680/1

MOSES DRAPER, COPP'S HILL, 1693

suitable for gravestones, and whenever a purchaser came and selected one, he left the inscription for it, and when several had been engaged, the man to letter them was sent for'; he adds that 'he faintly remembers some of these slabs standing against the front of the shop which stood across the street from the boulder.' Windsor and its neighborhood is full of this rather bright red sandstone — the oldest gravestones being usually only lettered.

A larger and more important quarry was that at Portland, with its lighter colored sandstone, almost a tan with deeper shades of chocolate. At Chatham, near Middletown, there was Johnson's quarry, worked by Thomas Johnson, who was born in 1689. He furnished the stone for the Hancock house in Boston in 1737. Shaler and Hall, his successors, advertised in 1781 to furnish any quantity for gravestones or monuments as well as for other purposes and 'deliver them at any Port in North America.'

Longmeadow, Massachusetts, also had quarries of red sandstone as well as many other smaller places in the Connecticut Valley. Apparently from one locality or another it was sent everywhere, and there are few burying-grounds where we do not find more or less of it. Contrary to popular belief, a fine quality is extremely enduring, and hundreds of sandstones to-day look as if the stonecutter had just laid down his chisel, as does that of William Wells Southold, 1696.

Many of the men who would naturally use sandstone in making gravestones seemed to prefer mica schist. There was a variety of it in Bolton, Connecticut, which, under the name of 'Bolton stone,' was very popular. Although it is always rather hard to decipher the inscriptions on this kind of a surface, it has a charm of its own, especially when on a late summer afternoon you stand on the burying-hill at Windham and see the gravestones all alight with the glow of the setting sun, seemingly garnished with all manner of precious stones and gold, as it were transparent glass, like the walls and streets of the New Jerusalem.

Marble gravestones or tombstones were not common until near the end of the eighteenth century. It was a great day for Newbury when in 1697, Colonel James Noyes discovered in that town the first body of limestone that had been found in Massachusetts. Sewall writes,
'Our

'Our Momford saith 'tis good marble.' Before that time all the lime was obtained from seashells, and we are not surprised that the people 'began to come with teams by thirty in a day' to carry off this valuable deposit. In King's Chapel Burying-Ground there is a little tomb of shell marble bearing the date 1702; this may have been of the Newbury marble. In some cases marble was imported, as in 1737, when Sir William Pepperell writes a letter to England ordering for his father 'a handsome marble tomb-stone with proper marble pillars or supporters to set it on.' This stone was to be engraved in England with the 'three pineapples proper' of the Pepperell family and was sent to Kittery, where it still can be seen opposite Sir William's old home. The bill was £34.11.4.

It was not until the western part of Massachusetts and Vermont were discovered to be desirable for dwelling-places that marble gravestones began to rival slate in number. The men who had spent their lives up to that time cutting the coarse red sandstones of the Connecticut Valley must have been delighted with this finer material, and their judgment that it was fitted for this purpose is seen to have been correct, when we wander into the marble burying-grounds, like those of Lanesboro, Massachusetts, and Bennington, Vermont, and see stones made in 1760 as untouched by time and weather as the slates and sandstones of more southern localities.

III. HOW GRAVESTONES WERE BOUGHT

Can we discover anywhere the simple business transaction of buying and paying for a gravestone? Here we turn to the Probate Registries. The very earliest records fail us in answering this question. Executors and administrators rendered no separate account until almost the close of the seventeenth century. The inventory of the estate usually ended with 'Debts due to the estate' and 'Debts due from the estate,' rarely itemized, and if they were, seldom giving more than the names of the debtors and creditors. The later records, however, from 1693, leaving aside all the doubtful cases in which one other than a stonecutter was paid for a gravestone or where a stonecutter was paid for other service, show a large number of cases where without any doubt a stonecutter was paid 'for gravestones.' We

cannot

ELIZABETH PROUT, COPP'S HILL, 1693/4

JOHN KNEELAND, ROXBURY, 1705(?)

GRACE BERRY, COPP'S HILL, 1695

SAMUEL RUGGLES, ROXBURY, 1692

cannot assume that every person who was so paid made the grave-stone. In some cases a wife or other near relative advanced the money to the estate, and in others there seems to have been a di-rector of the funeral ceremonies who assumed all the expenses, some-times 'including gravestones,' and sometimes, in a more itemized account, 'for gravestones.' Nor can we assume that even a well-known stonecutter, who receives a pound or two for an undesignated service, was necessarily paid for a gravestone. There were many other needs of the ordinary householder more pressing — slate hearths, sinks, doorsteps, various kinds of mason's work, and other possibilities in entirely different lines, all might appear on the exe-cutor's account. Even when we read that Hugh McDaniel in 1771 paid 'John Homer for a Grin stone,' and call to mind the grinning skulls that were John Homer's specialty, we are forced to the conclu-sion that the painstaking maker of this account intended no pun and ordered no gravestone.

Probably the men of those days, like those of to-day, carved their stones as they found the time and inspiration, and the customer selected from their limited stock the one that best pleased him and had it lettered to order. In one case, at least, the gravestone is on hand at the funeral. It may have been frequently done. Sewall writes on August 22, 1717, 'Mrs. Mary Winchcomb was buried in the old burying place in the 67th year of her age, as her relations tell me; though the stone bear 69.' And Mary Winchcomb's stone can still be read in King's Chapel Burying-Ground as Sewall read it the day of her funeral never corrected by her relations, 'dec'd Aug. 20th 1717 in the 69th year of her age.' In this case we see there were only two days between her sudden death and her funeral, time enough to let-ter a stone, but hardly enough to carve it.

An economical habit of our ancestors is responsible for some con-fusion in judging of the age of a stone — the habit of making-over things. They were brought up to turn their dresses and their carpets if they had any, to unrip the long center seam of a sheet and resew it with the outside edges together — in fact, life was a long lesson in getting the most out of their materials, and they did the same with their gravestones. Wandering through the old burying-grounds, we

occasionally

occasionally meet with an irrelevant inscription on some part of a stone, like that of Alexander Adams, Copp's Hill, 1677, which has the words 'Marston's Tomb' cut on the back.

More often our attention is arrested by a stone which we immediately recognize as belonging to a very early period, but carrying a much later date, like that of Mrs. Prudence Whitwell, the wife of the Reverend William, of Marblehead, who died in 1773. Her gravestone on Burial Hill was undoubtedly made in the seventeenth or very early eighteenth century. The work of erasing the early inscription has been done exceedingly well, but still by careful examination we can here and there catch a glimpse of it.

In Lexington, the stone of William Grimes, 1766, is in the very early style of the Lamsons, signed, as Caleb Lamson did fifty years before, 'C. L.' He was living when William Grimes died and may have sold an early specimen of his work, but more likely the stone had already done duty for one generation and was smoothed over and relettered for another. Here, too, the erasure is very well done, but the figure '8' under the 'N' in November is a bit suspicious and a careful examination shows other traces of the earlier inscription.

A still more notable example stands in old Newbury, where Elizabeth Greenleaf was interred in 1712. There are two other stones, that of Edward Grant, Copp's Hill, 1682, and Mary Barnes, King's Chapel, 1682, which have such a very close resemblance to this that we cannot doubt for a moment that it was from the same hand. There is, however, one very notable difference. The panel on Elizabeth's stone which bears the inscription has been planed down below the surface of the rest and still shows many marks of the chisel which did the work. Thirty years after the date of these other two, this one was relettered. Over the top are some Latin words cut by a different hand from the inscription. This newer man may also have added the narrow border across the bottom and chipped off the two pears to make a smoother surface to go under the sod.

We sometimes wonder why the people of these past days ever bought some of the gravestones; those that have a rather hideous death's-head, or are carelessly done with three or more rows of teeth, bad spelling, poor spacing, and made perhaps on a poor piece of
slate

JOSEPH TAPPING, KING'S CHAPEL, 1678

MARY CROMALL, SALEM, 1683

JOHN CARTER, WOBURN, 1692

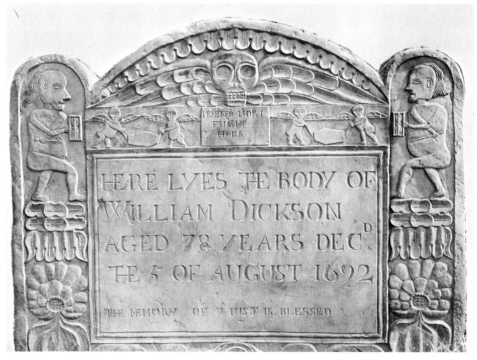

WILLIAM DICKSON, CAMBRIDGE, 1692

slate which broke under the stonecutter's tool. It is easy to forget that they had little or no choice. In the very large towns like Boston, there was more or less variety, but the majority lived in small towns, where they all had about the same things. They wove their own cloth, one piece very much like another; their pewter dishes were all very similar; even their rare ornaments and pictures were like those of their neighbors. When it came to gravestones, they ordered what they could get. If there was a local stonecutter near by, they may have visited his shop, but all his stones were much alike, and, even if they did not quite like them, they were the thing to have. If they had to send out of town, they probably all wrote a letter much like that of David Foster of Andover, quoted in Pierce's 'Foster Genealogy':

Mr. Robert Mulican of Bradford Ser pray make; for me Two Gravestones; one for David Foster jeunier of Andover; who died the 22;day of Dec; in the year of our Lord 1736, in the 20th year of his age; the son of David and Lidea Foster of Andover.

And one for Lidea Foster, the daughter of David and Lidea Foster of Andover; who died in the 17th year of her age in the year of our Lord 1736 and when they are made; send me word; and I will come and pay you for them.

DAVID FOSTER

And one for Isaac Foster; the son of Joshua and Mary Foster of Andover who died in the third year of her age in the year 1738. Pray send me word when it is made; and I will satisfie you for it

JOSHUA FOSTER

Let them all be made; before you send us word the 3rd day of April 1739.

Undoubtedly Robert Mulican made these three gravestones as well as his artistic sense and his working tools permitted, and David and Joshua Foster accepted and paid for them and were satisfied.

In 1769 the Reverend Peter Thacher, of Barnstable, went up to Dorchester to preach for a brother minister and took the opportunity to do his necessary shopping; on the succeeding Wednesday he writes, 'I paid for gravestones for my dear Bathsheba and sent them to Barnstable.' He probably selected on Monday what the stonecut-

ter

ter had to offer and had them lettered and paid for and sent two days later.

IV. THE STONECUTTERS

Having reached the conclusion that the majority of the early gravestones were carved in this country, some perhaps from slate which had come from England or Wales, more from native stone, and having seen how they were sold by the men who made them, the question naturally arises who were these men, what was their station in life, and what were their other occupations?

As we study the stones in the old burying-grounds, they gradually arrange themselves into groups. We can imagine we are entering various workshops, each containing the work of one man. It is not hard to distinguish little peculiarities, the expression of the death's-head, the shape of the hourglass and its wooden frame, the sweep of the wings, and the lettering of the inscription. Each style soon becomes like the handwriting of a friend.

When we have learned to recognize these various identification marks, we discover that the work of one man is fairly closely confined to a given locality. If living in a place of size and importance, he may occasionally send a stone to a fair distance, but usually, if we note the towns where his work most abounds, we shall find his own home is near their common center.

Again, those of a given style were apparently made within a lifetime. Where it seems almost too long for one active life, we need to remember that sometimes a number of years elapsed before an estate was settled and a grave marked. In this case the young stonecutter appears to have been too early a worker. His working years are also seemingly prolonged by the unfinished gravestones which he left at his death, and which may not have been sold immediately. It is not uncommon to have the widow credit herself with money received from such a source.

It would be comparatively easy to trace the early stonecutters had they been only stonecutters and employed only that title to describe themselves. But a man that could use his hands well in the early days of the settlement of New England usually did many things.

NICHOLAS CHATWELL, SALEM, 1700

JOHN MACKINTOSH, GRANARY, 1710

REV. JEREMIAH CUSHING, SCITUATE, 1705/6

WILLIAM MUMFORD, JR., COPP'S HILL, 1704

things. We should expect that the stonecutter might be also a mason, furnishing the foundations for buildings; and not far removed is the bricklayer, who worked with him on houses and chimneys; the slater, too, not only slated roofs, but also the sides of the buildings, made hearths and steps, and built tombs.

But in addition to these allied trades, there are certain crafts that we find very frequently combined with stonecutting. One is that of the cordwainer, the man who not only made and repaired the shoes for the community, but also did the more ornamental kinds of leather work. He made the big wallets carried by the men; the powder pouches, the saddles, and the chair seats, all of them requiring fine tooled work.

It is not uncommon to find that the man who made gravestones was also a surveyor who was used to laying out plans, running lines, and making maps.

It was easy for a brazier with his skilled use of tools to slip into stonecarving as did the engraver on wood. The woodcarver, too, might like to try his skill and patterns on this more enduring material, and we occasionally find a touch of this allied craft, as we do on the stone of Thomas Bancroft Wakefield, 1691.

We should expect that the stonecutter would be a farmer, and except in the larger towns he not only usually was, but often he hid his stonecutting trade under the exhaustive description of husbandman.

Here we find our great difficulty in placing the early stonecutters. How can we know that the masons, the bricklayers, cordwainers, tuckers, and braziers and the many husbandmen and yeomen might any one of them be also a stonecutter and a maker of gravestones? Nor can we assign them to the group of laborers who belonged to the lower social class.

In 'King Lear,' Shakespeare, only a few years before the thousands of artificers were settling in Massachusetts Bay, makes Cornwall ask, 'A tailor make a man?' And Kent answers, 'Aye, a tailor, Sir; a stonecutter or a painter could not have made him so ill, though he had been but two hours at the trade.' It seems that Shakespeare uses the designation of stonecutter as we might sculptor, a skillful man who could carve a likeness as the artist painted one.

As

As a matter of fact, we discover stonecutters in all walks of life, and again we meet a difficulty in recognizing them. How can we tell that a Gentleman, a Captain, a Deacon, a Representative to the General Court, or a Judge was also a stonecutter and a carver of gravestones?

V. SOURCES OF DESIGN

The very early stonecutters came possibly with designs, certainly with ideas, derived from stones which they had seen in the countries where they had lived. Some were from England; more from Scotland or Ireland; a few, perhaps, from Germany. They may have carved stone in their home country for churches or houses — for tombs or gravestones. Perhaps they brought with them notebooks with a pencil sketch of some border or figure which they liked — a poor equipment for work in a land where there were no libraries, no museums, no teachers of art.

It is not surprising that the very earliest stones show scarcely any ornamentation — a simple rosette, cross-bones, hourglass, a narrow border, usually without relief, was all they attempted. It was not many years, however, before the elaborate scrolls and the garlands of fruit, urns and flowers, all in high-relief, succeeded these modest designs.

Where did they get these new ideas and the new impetus for more elaborate and beautiful work? Undoubtedly skilled craftsmen of all kinds were constantly being added to New England's population, and perhaps they brought with them drawings or prints of work which was being done in the countries from which they came. But it does not seem to be these new men who actually carved the elaborate stones. The impetus for more expensive gravestones undoubtedly came from the greater wealth of the country, and the old stonecutters and their native-born apprentices rose equal to the demand.

By 1678 there seems to have been a choice of woodcarvers in Boston, for in October of that year the General Court 'ordered to be forthwith carved by an able artist the King's Arms,' which were to be 'errected in the Court House.'

Woodcarving would seem to be more nearly allied to stonecarving
than

NATHANAEL MATHER, SALEM, 1688

HENRY SEWALL, NEWBURY, 1700

ANN MUMFORD, NEWPORT, 1697/8

THADDEUS MACCARTY, GRANARY, 1705

than any other craft, and it may be quite possible that the man who could make a satisfactory coat-of-arms and realistic lions and unicorns might have a well-filled portfolio of scrolls and leaves of varying shapes and flowers and fruits of all kinds.

Beautiful old pieces of furniture, too, were coming over in every vessel: solid oak chairs with elaborate scrolls and the initials of the owner or the date, on the back; chests often quite covered with figures and borders and arabesques, like that of Michael Metcalf brought over by him in 1637 and still a thing of beauty, in the rooms of the Dedham Historical Society. It was not only the joiner of that day who could find his inspiration in these pieces of furniture; the stonecutter, too, with an eye trained to seize on anything that might help his art, could adapt their beauty to his purpose.

Other trades may have helped. Almost all the stonecutters had some other occupation which they followed as industriously as that of stonecarving. The cordwainer may have found some bit of Spanish leather, curiously tooled, which suggested a new curve for his scroll; the brazier in some imported vessel of copper or brass may have discovered a bird or queer Babylonish figure which he could appropriate; even the 'Japanner' could select something of value from his illuminated boxes and trays.

Occasionally we come across a gravestone which apparently had its inspiration in some untutored mind — perhaps borrowed from the pottery of our native Indians or the blankets they wore. One such stone is that of Joseph Larned, Putnam, Connecticut, 1756.

The printer, too, with his head and tail pieces, his ornate borders, and especially his clear-cut letters, must have been a source of inspiration.

It is interesting to note that, however many ideas the stonecutters absorbed from all these different sources, they made them their own. They not only never seemed to copy another man's work; they never copied their own. Stones that were replicas of each other do not appear until the middle of the eighteenth century. Each early stone is individual, the flowers, acanthus and laurel leaves and fruit, arranged as the fancy of the sculptor dictated, with a freedom from set patterns which seems extraordinary when we realize that he had so little pre-
cedent

cedent and so little suggestion outside his own fertile brain. This constant variety in detail shows that the stonecarver loved his work — that his mind was always alert for a more pleasing way of presenting the old thoughts to the people of his day.

CHAPTER III
THE SEVENTEENTH-CENTURY STONECUTTERS OF BOSTON

THERE must have been many stonecutters among the artificers and handicraftsmen who came in great numbers to Boston in the seventeenth century. As we have already seen, most of them had some other trade. Occasionally we discover a name of some one of them — among the earliest are William White, who left his stonecutting tools with tools for various other purposes to his two sons; Henry Stevens, said to have been a stonemason; Elias Grice and William Parham, Jr., both called stonecutters in the deeds of Suffolk County. Some of these, or none of them, may have made gravestones. There are, however, three workers of that early period who stand out from the others and who must have been pre-eminent in their line. The earliest of them was a man called 'The Stone Cutter of Boston,' and contemporaneous with the later period of his work were William Mumford and J. N.

'THE STONE CUTTER OF BOSTON

The Reverend Zachariah Symmes, of Charlestown, died on February 4, 1670. A year or two later the following action was taken by the Town:

> In pursuance of a Town order the 6.11.72 that a tomb of Stone should be erected over the grave of Mr. Zachariah Symmes deceased, It is ordered that the three deacons and Lawrence Hammond do treat and conclude with the stone cutter at Boston for a meet stone for that use; and that John Goodwin or Sam Bickner or some other mason be agreed with to build a stone work laid in lime, over the grave as soon as the weather will permit, and that the three deacons be desired to see the same issued with all convenient speed.

From the wording of this order we are forced to the conclusion that if there was more than one stonecutter in Boston at that time, he was of slight consequence, and one alone was worthy to be called 'The Stonecutter.'

The Town Treasurer paid:

To

To a tombstone and a burying cloth for ye Towne	12.0.0
To bush. lime	0.10.0
To carting ye Stone to ye Grave by Thos. Welch	0.16.0

Thomas Welch was at that time a young man of seventeen; later he made gravestones himself and very likely carted the stones to the grave because he was an apprentice of 'The Stone Cutter of Boston.' As there is no further charge for engraving the stone, it is fair to conclude that it came all ready to take its place above the tomb which John Goodwin or Sam Bickner had built. Like many of the horizontal slabs in Charlestown, no inscription can now be read upon it, and therefore no clue is furnished to this man's work.

Judge Sewall also fails us. Full as is his diary of the names of both the great and small Boston folk of his day, his one entry about a stonecutter reads: 'May 4 1687, I spend a pretty deal of time in the burying place to see to the Graver of the Tombstone' — time wasted as far as posterity is concerned, for the only inscription now upon his tomb was cut by some other 'Graver' more than a hundred years after the day when he 'saw to' the earlier workman.

There are many gravestones in and around Boston which apparently were all done by one man, possibly helped by his sons or apprentices, none of them signed, but all bearing the stamp of the same individuality. One of the earliest is the very old, badly scaled and stained stone of Ann Erinton, Cambridge, 1653. Its only ornamentation is a simple, beautifully cut rosette, still crisp and clear, as is the inscription.

There are few New England gravestones in existence as old as this, and we have to jump a period of nearly twenty years before we find other work which we can attribute to the same hand. Then we discover here and there other rosettes like Ann Erinton's, not enough, however, for us to conclude that the man who carved them would merit the distinction of being 'The Stone Cutter.' In fact another quite different design is much more abundant. Everywhere we see it. It is not very showy, usually only an oddly shaped head, very full, with plenty of room for brains, the eyebrows commonly ending in a little hook, a broad jaw with a generous supply of teeth, and wings coming well up over the ears having feathers often arranged in

two

SARAH NISBETT, MILFORD, CONN., 1698

REV. EDWARD TOMPSON, MARSHFIELD, 1705

DEBORAH THOMAS, MARSHFIELD, 1696

two or three tiers. Accompanying this head are simple symbols of death, the hourglass, and cross-bones, the pickaxe and spade, perchance a coffin, and often a few words of Latin. Phinehas Pratt, Charlestown, 1680, 'one of the first English inhabitants of ye Massachusetts Colony,' has a stone of this style and shows the neat lettering with the *t*'s like crescents.

Although we find stones which we cannot assign to this man, those that we do recognize as his exceed in quantity the output of all the other very early stonecutters — so much so that it seems almost certain that we have discovered the work of 'The Stone Cutter.' Just as we reach this conclusion, we find in Charlestown the stone that John and Martha Cutler erected to the memory of their three children in 1680, which still, very badly stained with smoke and grime, is in the Phipps Street Burying-Ground. On this is carved Ann Erinton's rosette, with no variation from type, and with it the curious characteristic death symbol, flattened a little at the top to make room for *fugit hora*, and letters and figures quite similar to those we have already seen.

There is little doubt that the man who carved Ann Erinton's stone in 1653 was the same man who also made those of Phinehas Pratt, the Cutler children, and innumerable others more or less like them.

Quite near the grave of the Cutler children in Charlestown is that of their grandmother, Anna Cutler. This, in addition to the well-known death symbol and the rosettes like the center of Ann Erinton's, has a new feature, a border, rather simple, and yet original in its treatment.

Anna Cutler is one of the few women who made an honorable entrance into the 'Magnalia,' for the Reverend Cotton Mather felt there was something supernatural in her last hours which was worthy of record. He writes:

Mr. J. C. deacon of the church in Charlestown told me that his wife having been sick for several months, was on the thirty-first of August last seiz'd with the pangs of death; in which being delirious and asking divers times who would go with her whither she was going? at length she said Well my son Robert will go, and addressing her speech therefrom as unto him, she expressed her satisfaction that they should go together. This son of hers was at that time in Barbadoes; and his friends here have since

learned

learned that he also dy'd there and this at the very hour when his mother here gave up the ghost; and (which is further odd) not without the like expression concerning his mother, that his mother had concerning him.

Mary Blackmore was buried in Charlestown in 1671. Her stone shows the hand of 'The Stone Cutter,' and in addition to what we recognize as his are the little men carrying the pall. These were later used very often by a man who must have learned his art from this early stonecutter, Joseph Lamson.

Thomas Rand, Charlestown, 1683, has the same odd winged death's-head gazing into space with very round and hollow eyes, but in addition there is a head used as a finial for each border. I have found many heads like these with the hair in scallops, and the straight mouth. A still more elaborate fruit border is carved on the stone of Rebekah Row, Charlestown, 1680 — that very appropriately named woman whose sad story Sewall tells us as follows:

Feb'y 24 1680/1 This morn the Wife of Mr. Elias Row is found dead in her bed; much blood about her, so some think she was choaked with it. A Jury was impanneled and six grave matrons and a chirugeon, to view the Corps to see if any violence had been offered her; found none; she and her husband seldom lay together; she was given to drink and quarreling. Her death puts in mind the proverb wherein we say such an one hath drunk more than he hath bled to-day.

Possibly Elias found when she was gone that after all she was dear to him in spite of her sharp tongue and so erected to her memory this very elaborate stone. He survived her only six years, and they lie near together in the Phipps Street Burying-Ground, but not side by side. His stone probably was also by 'The Stone Cutter,' but by 1686 Joseph Lamson was working independently and it is hard to distinguish the work of the two men.

Epitaphs often help in identifying the carver of a gravestone. Undoubtedly many of them were written by the ministers or other friends of the deceased. Collecting them in the seventeenth century was as common as collecting 'antiques' is to-day, with the difference that in those olden times it was the man who collected; women had no time for such matters. We catch a glimpse of Sewall and Cotton Mather in 1696, after the funeral of 'Brother Pemberton' and a 'good

RUTH CARTER, GRANARY, 1697/8

MATTHEW PITTOM, COPP'S HILL, 1693/4

REV. ICHABOD WISWALL, DUXBURY, 1700

THOMAS WADE, IPSWICH, 1696

'good dinner,' strolling through the old graveyard at Cambridge and Mather's 'taking off' the epitaphs of the Reverends Chauncy and Oakes while Sewall read them to him.

However many epitaphs were furnished the stonecutter, he must often have been left to his own devices, when, in addition to the name, necessary relationships, and date of death, he had an opportunity to add a touch of his own, and 'The Stone Cutter of Boston' always chose a bit of Latin. He had many ways of saying, 'Remember Death.' One way, '*Dies Tenebrarium Memento*,' was not very frequently used; by far the oftenest was the simple '*Memento Mori*,' which perhaps the women and children could understand, and fairly often, '*Vive Memento loethi*,' a line from Persius — a Latin author we have forgotten to-day and have almost forgotten that *lethus* is an old word for death. But 'The Stone Cutter' knew his Latin, especially his Ovid, from which he chose many an appropriate thought. On the stone of the Neal children, Granary, 1671, he has engraved the words, '*Tempus edax rerum*.' Perhaps he was once a college boy and sang '*Lauriger Horatius*,' and perhaps he knew these Latin words were not written by Horace as the college boys of to-day might affirm. Another of his favorites was '*Memento te esse mortalem*.'

On Joseph Farnum's stone, Copp's Hill, 1678, he again quotes from Ovid:

> '*Ultima semper*
> *Expectanda dies homine dicique beatus*
> *Ante obitum supremaque funera debit*.'

(The last day must always be awaited by man and no one should be called happy before his death and final funeral rites.)

Also in Copp's Hill is the temperamental stone of Elizabeth Prout, who died in 1693, 'after sore conflicts of mind,' as Sewall tells us, and 'not without suspicion of witchcraft.' Her husband, Timothy, was for many years Boston's Town Clerk. The first thing that strikes our eye, as we catch sight of it, is the fact that, among all the gray and black stones around it, it alone is almost a pure white. I wondered, when I started to photograph it, whether the lettering and design would come out more distinctly if it were wet. Trying the experiment,

periment, I found to my great surprise that the whole became as black as the others. A few minutes of sunlight made it again that very unusual thing, a white slate — perhaps after all these years a vindication of Elizabeth's suspected character. The whiteness seems to be caused by a microscopic fungus or deposit, but it is not so easy to understand why the fungus should choose to grow almost exclusively on the stone of Elizabeth Prout.

We find 'The Stone Cutter's' work in all the old burying-grounds near Boston. It covers a long period, from 1653 to 1695. The majority of his stones have little ornamentation, but sometimes he attempted more ambitious effects. Perhaps his masterpiece is in Dorchester, the stone of John Foster, 1681. We might not recognize it as his had we not already seen the very similar stone for Joseph Tapping, King's Chapel, which has more that is characteristic of his work than this later one.

John Foster was a son of Hopestill and Mary Bates Foster, born in 1648. Although only thirty-three at the time of his death, he had lived a full life. When twenty-one he had engraved a portrait of the Reverend Richard Mather; he was the first printer in Boston; he compiled one of the early almanacs; and he had engraved the seal of Massachusetts. He had written a book about comets and knew much astronomy. Besides all this, if we can judge from his inventory, there were other things he liked to do. He owned turning tools and carving tools, and 'cutts and colors,' also a 'Gitturn viol' and 'weather glasses'; he certainly crowded much into his short life, and when he died he requested in his will that twenty or thirty shillings should be 'paid or reserved for a pair of handsome Gravestones.' His brothers must have tried to select the best man they could find to make them, and they saw how very appropriate to him would be a design similar to that on Joseph Tapping's stone, standing then as now in the burying-ground of King's Chapel.

One of the favorite pastimes of this early period was the making of anagrams — seeing what could be spelt out of the letters of a friend's name. From John Foster's they evolved, 'I shone forth,' rather appropriate for a man as fond of the heavenly bodies as he. Possibly the sculptor had this in mind when he added, to the design

he

PETER TUFTS, MALDEN, 1700

JOHN HAMMOND, WATERTOWN, 1709

SAMUEL FLETCHER, CHELMSFORD, 1704/5

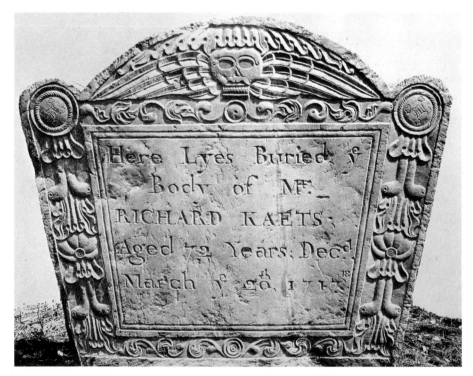

RICHARD KAETS, CONCORD, 1717/8

he had already used for Joseph Tapping, a midday sun with shining rays.

When it was known that John Foster had not long to live, Increase Mather sent him a Latin verse which has been translated — 'Living thou studiest the stars; dying, mayst thou Foster, I pray, mount above the skies and learn to measure the highest heaven.' Foster bravely writes back, 'I measure it and it is mine; the Lord Jesus has bought it for me; nor am I held to pay aught for it but thanks.' These couplets signed with the initials I. M. and J. F. were cut upon his headstone.

No wonder when he died Increase Mather wrote, 'a great loss to the country.'

Elegiacs and poems were written about him:

> 'His piercing Astronomic eye
> Could penetrate the cloudy sky
> And soar aloft i'th highest sphere
> Descrying stars that disapper
> To common eyes. But Faith and Hope
> His all excelling telescope,
> Did help his heaven-born soul to pry
> Beyond the starry canopy.'

'The Stone Cutter' carved upon the headstone whatever he was asked to do, but the footstone was left free for him to inscribe as he pleased, and what could be more appropriate for such a talented young man than a line from his favorite Ovid, '*Ars illi sua census erat*'? and underneath he kindly translates it for us, 'Skill was his cash.'

In Salem there is a beautiful gravestone with the same kind of scroll as there is on John Foster's. It is that of 'Mary Cromall,' 1683. Mary was one of the four wives of Philip Cromwell, the butcher whose first wife refused to come to New England, 'being very comfortably situated where she was.' He married for his third wife Mary, the widow of Robert Lemon. Whatever may have been Philip's failings, he had good taste in gravestones, as his own and this of his wife still testify.

Very similar to this, not only in the style of engraving, but also in the

the rather unusual shape of the stone, is that of Grace Berry, Copp's Hill, 1695 — the latest one I have found which has the quality of 'The Stone Cutter's' work, possibly lettered by some one else, but the scrolls, with their pointed leaves and the round-headed death symbol, leave us little doubt that we are looking upon almost the last work from this master's hand.

WILLIAM MUMFORD

To be at once a Quaker and a maker of gravestones indicates independence and originality.

The first mention we have of William Mumford is in the will of Henry Shrimpton, brazier of Boston, where he leaves £5 to 'my servant William Mumford if he then live with me.' He was at that time a young man about twenty-five, and perhaps in the brazier's shop he learned to engrave on brass and copper, a good preparation for the work he was later to do.

Henry Shrimpton died soon after, in 1666, and with his death William Mumford struck out boldly into a new manner of living. He probably received the five pounds, for not long afterwards we find him married and comfortably established at the North End. He bought from Jonathan Copp sometime before 1676, the old house built and occupied by the father, William Copp, and without much doubt he had married Ruth Copp, William's daughter. Ruth Copp was born September 24, 1643. By the terms of her father's will she was to receive ten pounds and also ten acres of land 'a little beyond Braintree,' a very good inheritance in those days, especially for a stone cutter, for Braintree was noted for its slate. The date of their marriage was not recorded, but their first child was born in 1671.

The Copp house must have been a fairly commodious one, for in 1676 the Mumfords sold one half of it with a patch of garden land to Samuel Saxton, a brickburner, but as long as Mumford lived William Copp's old house, or at least a part of it, seems to have been his home and Copp's Hill with its burying-ground his special care and joy.

His wife, Ruth, was a member of the Mather Church, and there all the children of 'Sister Ruth Mumford' were baptized. William Mumford himself was a Quaker, and he boldly steps into the limelight in

August,

JOHN FOWLE, CHARLESTOWN, 1711

MARY ROUS, CHARLESTOWN, 1714/5

MARY ROGERS, BILLERICA, 1697

JOSEPH LAMSON, CHARLESTOWN, 1722

August, 1677, when he attends a Quaker meeting in Boston — a very deliberate act, because only a week or two previously this same group of worshipers had been arrested while at their devotions and all but two publicly whipped through the streets. Of the fifteen present at this second meeting, nine of them had attended the earlier one and had braved another encounter with the Boston constables, and six new persons had joined them, William Mumford among the number. A like fate awaited them, as doubtless they expected. To them was meted out the public whipping which they had coveted.

For this bit of history, Snow, who wrote the 'History of Boston,' in 1825, states that he was indebted 'to a venerable professor of the denomination.'

I have discovered nothing of William Mumford's ancestry. There is a letter in existence from James Claypole, a Friend, which would seem to fix his English home in Worcestershire. This letter is written to John Spread and is as follows:

London the 29.7th. mo. 1681. I am earnestly desired by a friend of mine in Worcestershire to make Inquiry for one William Mumford, a stone cutter in Boston whether he be living or not, if living that in thy next Letter he may write a few lines and it may be attested by some that comes over in the next ship to end a law sute for one that holds an estate during his life.

There seems to be no relationship between William Mumford and the family of Mountforts in Boston, although the two names are interchangeable. There were, however, Mumfords in Rhode Island, Quakers and Seventh-Day Baptists, who may have been relatives, as will appear when we examine their gravestones.

Evidently by 1681, when John Spread wrote his letter from London, William Mumford was well known as a stonecutter. He is also called mason and slater. Probably he worked gradually into the finer parts of the business, not really coming into the front rank of gravestone-makers until after the death, or at least the retiring from work, of 'The Stone Cutter of Boston.'

In the meantime he was an exceedingly busy man in other ways. He, with three of his friends at the North End, John Comer, a pewterer, James Smith, a shopkeeper, and Joshua Hewes, an innkeeper, and half a dozen people whom they called their partners, bought,

sometime

sometime before 1684, from John Wampus, Indian, a tract of land in the Nipmuck Country, which afterwards became the Town of Sutton. This land was confirmed unto them by the General Court, with the single condition that they should render and pay unto their Sovereign Lady Queen Anne and her successors, 'one fifth part of all the gold and silver oar and Precious stones' that they might discover.

Their names all appear on the first pages of the Sutton history, but Sutton has forgotten them — all but one. She remembers Mumford, for in the southern part of the town Mumford River still furnishes power for her mills, and near it, over the line in what is now Douglas, is Mumford Street.

Another enterprise which must have taken much of his time was done for the Quakers. However much they as a class disapproved of his work in commemorating the dead, they found in him their chief moving spirit and the most energetic member of their Society. To him they owed their place in the community. In 1694 he bought a large lot of land on Brattle Street and built for them a meeting-house, said to be the first brick meeting-house in Boston erected for 'the service and worship of Almighty God.' When some years later the Society outgrew this building, it was Mumford who bought another lot of land and built them another church and around it laid out their plain burying-ground, from which, in 1826, more than a hundred bundles of bones were carried to Lynn.

William Mumford is the first person whose name I have found in the Suffolk Probate Records as having been paid for a gravestone. In 1693, during the terrible scourge of yellow fever which visited Boston, Moses Draper died, 'a very hopefull young man' according to Sewall, and his estate paid 'Mr. Mumford for Gravestones 1.0.0.' The modest stone which this amount of money bought in 1695 still stands in Copp's Hill Burying-Ground.

Captain Samuel Ruggles, of Roxbury, had died a short time before Moses Draper, and there is little doubt that the item in his executor's account which reads, 'To Mr. Mumford, Stone Cutter 1.0.0.' was for the stone which still marks his grave in the Eustis Street Burying-Ground. It has been wonderfully well preserved, from both weather

and

DEANE WINTHROP, REVERE, 1703/4

MARY CUTLER, CHARLESTOWN, 1703

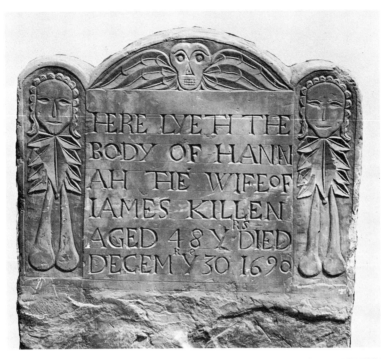

HANNAH KILLEN, CHARLESTOWN, 1696

REV. JONATHAN PIERPONT, WAKEFIELD, 1709

and human depredations, watched over doubtless by the same guardian spirit which protected the Captain in his lifetime. For he, thirty
years before his death, had been the subject of a 'Remarkable Providence,' when going up Meeting-House Hill; he was 'struck by
lightning, his two oxen and horse killed, a chest in the cart with
goods in it burned in Sundry places, himself coming off the cart
carried twenty feet from it yet no abiding hurt.'

I think it is quite safe to say that the stone at the grave of Elias
Grice in the Granary is also the work of William Mumford. Elias
Grice was a young man, only twenty-eight when he died, but he is
described as a stonecutter, and he and William Mumford bought
land together which would indicate some kind of partnership. He
died in 1684 and his brother Josiah, who died in 1690 lies buried at
his side with a stone exactly like that of Elias. It is possible that the
two stones were put up at the same time by Josiah's executor, which
would make them only a little older than those of Moses Draper and
Samuel Ruggles.

Turning again to the Probate records of Suffolk County, we find
the first mention of William Mumford is in the settlement of John
Hayward's estate in 1688/9, possibly for a gravestone, possibly for
some other service. It is not until about 1700 that his name appears
quite frequently, often as 'the stone cutter.'

In 1700, Nicholas Chatwell, of Salem, died, and in the settlement
of his estate it appears that Mr. Josiah Wolcott, 'a Boston Man,' was
paid 'for Momford's account 0.24.0.' Nicholas Chatwell's gravestone
is still to be seen in the Charter Street Burying-Ground.

John Kneeland, of Roxbury, died in 1691, but it was not until
1721, at the time of the settlement of the estate of his son John, that
we find a mention of a gravestone to his memory. The item reads,
'To two pair Gravestones for Father, Mother and sister of William
Mumford 2.0.0.' Mother's and sister's headstone has disappeared,
but father's, rather poorly cut, is still in the Eustis Street Burying-
Ground, probably purchased by John Kneeland some years after his
father's death, as the mother, Mary Kneeland, appears on the footstone as Mary Henway. Ruth, the sister, lived until 1705. This
stone of John Kneeland has the same design as that of little Mary
Mumford,

Mumford, Copp's Hill, 1677/8, without much doubt a daughter of the stonecutter.

There is one other stone which must be his, that of his only son William, Copp's Hill, 1704, a queer twisted stone with a lowering, malevolent death symbol having a border such as we find often on stones of that period, possibly all by Mumford.

Studying these six stones we can get an idea of the kind of work which he did, and from them can assign to him many others, some of them much more elaborate and doubtless more expensive than those these prudent executors ordered from the slender estates they had to distribute.

With the single exception of the stone of William Mumford, Jr., his death symbol is always round-eyed and calm, looking with untroubled vision at the passer-by. Death to this Quaker carver was not to be dreaded; it rather foretold the peace and happiness of the life beyond, until it came for his own son, when, by changing the shape of the eyes and lowering the forehead, he expressed a terrible, unwelcome death. In all of them, except this, the teeth are rather carefully cut and are nearly if not quite opposite each other, and the nose is formed by two triangles one within the other. On most of his stones we can see very faint lines where the slate had been carefully ruled, the rosettes at the tops of the side borders are simple discs or coils, and the lettering, entirely in capitals, is in the same style on each stone. 'The' is always written 'ye,' and each inscription begins, 'Here lyes' or 'Here lyeth.'

Among the many stones with a pattern similar to that of William Mumford, Jr., we find one in Scituate — that of the Reverend Jeremiah Cushing, 1705/6, which has all these characteristics with the addition of faces in the side discs.

More elaborate still is the stone in Newbury which Judge Sewall erected to the memory of his parents in 1700, with a long inscription which we know from his diary he wrote himself. We should expect Sewall would choose Mumford to make this stone — he knew him well, living as he did almost adjoining Sewall's land at the North End, and having made gravestones for very many of his best friends. In one place he speaks of him as 'Our Mumford.'

On

HERE LYES Y
BODY OF LYDIA WOOD
WIFE TO JOSIAH
WOOD AGED 74
YEARS DIED NOUEM.R
Y 25.R 1712

LYDIA WOOD, CHARLESTOWN, 1712

Here Lyes y
Body of Cap
pyam Blower
Aged 71 year
Who Departed
This Life
june The 1st
1 7 0 9
in Their Death Thay

Also Here Lyes
y Body of Mrs
Elizabeth Blower
The Wife of Cap
pyam Blower
Aged 69 years
Who Departed
This Life May
The 29 1709
Ware Not Diuided

CAPTAIN AND MRS. BLOWER, CAMBRIDGE, 1709

MARY REED, MARBLEHEAD, 1712/3

JONATHAN REMINGTON, CAMBRIDGE, 1738

On this stone we find all Mumford's characteristics — the very delicate ruling both above and below the lettering, which is in capitals, the cheerful death symbol, with teeth meeting squarely, and the simple discs.

This epitaph was written in 1701, when the Judge's heart was sadly disturbed by the attitude of the Reverend Cotton Mather against him, who 'came to Mr. Wilkins shop and there talked very sharply against me as if I had used his father worse than a neger, spoke so loud that people in the street might hear him. Then went and told Sam [Sewall's son] that one pleaded much for Negros and he had used his father worse that a Negro and that was his father. I had read in the morn Mr. Dod's saying Sanctified Afflictions are good promotions. I found it now a cordial. And this caused me the rather to set under my Father and Mother's epitaph Ps. 27 10. "When my Father and Mother forsake me, then the Lord will take me up."' And then Sewall remembers that a week or so earlier he had sent 'Mr. Increase Mather a haunch of very good venison,' and adds, 'I hope in that I did not treat him as a Negro.'

It would seem that the Mathers would select William Mumford as their family stonecutter. He lived very near them, his wife attended their church, and they baptized his children. So we are not surprised to find that the stone of Nathanael Mather, Salem, 1688, bears a close resemblance to that of Henry Sewall. Nathanael Mather was son of the Reverend Increase. We are told by the Reverend John Higginson that 'his piety and learning was beyond his years.'

Ipswich has many stones which are more like William Mumford's work than that of any other stonecutter of that period. Colonel Thomas Wade, 1696, has the real Mumford death's-head, a close double to that on Henry Sewall's stone, and lettering which is nearly identical with his. The border of Thomas Wade's is much more beautiful and perhaps shows Mumford at his best.

In the Common Burying-Ground, on Farewell Street in Newport, there is a row of interesting stones placed in memory of the Newport Mumfords. William Mumford seems to have always been in touch with Newport; he had real estate transactions with Newport men, his daughter Elizabeth, the only child of his who, as far as we know,

was

was married, lived in Newport with her husband, Edward Rossam. It is not surprising to find in this burying-ground stones which seem to have been made by this Boston stonecutter, as, for instance, that of Ann Mumford, 1697/8. Surely its death's-head greets us with the very same cheerful expression we have seen so many times in Copp's Hill and the Granary. Strangely enough, too, just touching the graves of these Newport Mumfords lie the children of Edward and Elizabeth Rossam, William Mumford's grandchildren. Were they related to Ann and Stephen Mumford or was it chance or friendship that led them to make their last beds together?

On November 21, 1718, William Mumford died. He chose to be buried on Copp's Hill rather than with the Quakers, who desired no stones to mark their graves. He was in good company, too. Nicholas Upshal and his wife, who suffered much on behalf of the Quakers; John Soames, too, one of the founders of their church and also a companion of William Mumford on the eventful day of the public whipping forty-one years before; the daughter of Eliphal Graves, another of that band, and many more Friends were waiting there for the General Resurrection.

His widow, Ruth, and her three living daughters chose to mark his grave with a large double stone of Connecticut sandstone. In spite of the coarseness of the material, it resembles his work, and may have been made by him for himself and his wife, but Ruth's name has never been cut upon it. Perhaps she went to Newport and may be buried near the other Mumfords on Farewell Street.

J. N.

In the old burying-ground on Hancock Street, in Quincy, there is a very unique and beautiful gravestone. Carved upon it are two peacocks facing each other below the usual death's-head. They are separated by an hourglass, which has engraved over it the initials 'J. N.' Whoever J. N. may have been, it is evident that he considered this stone his masterpiece, and he wished it remembered that he made it, for on the hourglass itself he has also placed the same initials, first on the upper part reading 'J. N.,' and again on the lower, reading this time 'N. J.,' a suggestion that on the back of the hourglass

the

ABIGAIL CODMAN, HAVERHILL, 1775

MARY ROBINSON, DUXBURY, 1722

Here Lyes y Body of
Mrs MARY ROBINSON,
Daugtr of y Revrd Mr JOHN
ROBINSON of Duxbury
& Mrs HANNAH His Wife,
Drowned wth her Mother,
in ye paſſage from Duxbury
to Boſton, Septr 22, 1722
Ætatis 16.
Then are they quiet because
they are at Reſt Pſl. 107 30.

JAMES FOSTER, DORCHESTER, 1763

PRISCILLA FOSTER, DORCHESTER, 1739

the lettering was continued, so if we could walk around it we should find four 'J. N.'s — five in all.

Who was J. N.? So far I have discovered no stonecutter of that period bearing these initials. No J. N. was paid for gravestones in the settlement of any estate in Suffolk or Middlesex County.

A man who would put his initials so many times on one stone would without doubt sign others, and such proves to be the case.

In Marshfield we find a beautiful stone over the grave of the Reverend Edward Tompson. It is cut with the same originality and freedom as the Peacock stone, and like that bears at the top of the curve the letters 'J. N.' It, too, is unique with its vase of flowers and borders made of large lilies.

On the footstone is one of those interesting epitaphs written without doubt by some brother minister:

> 'anno aetatis suae 40
> Here in a Tyrant's Hand does captive lye
> A rare Synopsis of Divinity
> Old Patriarchs, prophets, Gospel Bishops meet
> Under deep silence in their winding sheet
> Here rest awhile in hopes and full intent
> When their King calls, to meet in Parliament.'

In Duxbury we discover another stone, quite different from the other two and signed 'J. N.' in script below the left-hand border. It is that of the Reverend Ichabod Wiswall, a man 'famous as an astrologer.'

Besides these three large stones there are several smaller ones also bearing the initials 'J. N.,' all of nearly the same period. They are those of Martha Hall, Roxbury, 1701; Sarah Dolbeare, Copp's Hill, 1701; and Mehitable Hammond, Newton, 1704. These small stones add little to our information about J. N.'s work. None of them have lilies or vases, but resemble in general conception that of the Reverend Ichabod Wiswall.

Discarding them, we will get what characteristics we can from the three larger and more typical stones, those of John Cleverly, of Quincy, Edward Tompson, of Marshfield, and Ichabod Wiswall, of Duxbury.

The

The earliest of the three is that of Ichabod Wiswall, 1700, while John Cleverly's and Edward Tompson's are 1703 and 1704 respectively — all done within a period of four years.

Ichabod Wiswall's is quite different from the other two and the signature is less conspicuous. We note the ruling for the general design, the odd shape of the figs, the extremely low forehead of the death's-head and the alternating teeth. The lettering, though more carelessly done, shows some of the peculiarities of the other two stones, the crossing of the *E*'s and *F*'s with a triangle, the prominent serifs, and the *U*'s always made as we make them to-day and not like the very common *V* of that day.

The other two stones have a strong resemblance to each other, both showing a remarkable freedom of treatment and great originality.

With these three stones as clues to J. N.'s work, we discover many others which we feel sure must have been carved by him.

In Marshfield, very near the grave of the Reverend Edward Tompson, is that of Deborah Thomas, and on her stone are the same large lilies that are depicted on his, the same rounded heavy stems, and the rosettes, under which the scrolls end, are in both cases flat discs used as a kind of background to an ornamental figure. Deborah, however, has a very new feature, a winged head with carefully arranged hair, the feathers of the wings being continued under her chin.

Although these signed stones are all south of Boston, it is in Boston itself that there are the greatest number of stones which resemble J. N.'s work.

Thaddeus Maccarty, Granary, 1705, has the very rounded scrolls of John Cleverly, the platelike rosettes of Edward Tompson, and, on the flowered top, the strongest resemblance to J. N. The central flower is one of his lilies with seven petals as Edward Tompson has, and the other flowers have the delicately crossed centers, also like his.

Not far from Thaddeus Maccarty is the stone of Ruth Carter; her vase is very much like Tompson's as is her scroll work and her lily. She, however, has a very new and very startling feature — two skeletons, carved by a skillful hand. Ordinarily one sufficed. Per-

haps

BACK OF TOMBSTONE OF REV. ANDREW ELIOT, COPP'S HILL

THANKFUL BAKER, DORCHESTER, 1697/8

JOSEPH NIGHTINGALE, QUINCY, 1715

STEPHEN WILLIAMS, ROXBURY, 1720

haps one of these depicts her as she lay in her coffin; the other, walking away with an upraised hand and a jaunty air as if, freed from confinement, she was going forth for new life and new work. Probably the boxes on which these skeletons stand represent the coffin. The lily springing from the vase with its wealth of foliage may be simply ornamental or it may symbolize the glorified Ruth blooming in the Garden of God.

As we have seen, J. N. was fond of lilies. Either he had a greater stock of imagination than any other contemporary stonecutter, or he had different sources of inspiration. Did he have some other vocation where scrolls, arabesques, unusual plants, and strange beings took him out of the beaten paths of gravestone ornamentation into fields of fancy? Could he have been a cordwainer, working on leather, and sometimes handling rare Spanish pieces with gay designs? Or was he a joiner who gave much of his time to bringing beauty in furniture or in interior finish to the few wealthy folk of the day and perhaps often mending some choice old chest or chair carved by skillful hands in the mother country?

Whatever his other occupation, it would seem as if he might have been the carver of a rather exotic style of gravestone, peculiar, as far as I know, to Boston or its near vicinity — a design which we might call the 'Urn and Mermaid.' I have found fourteen of these stones.

Leaving the interpretation of this extraordinary representation to another chapter, I will here suggest a few points of resemblance between the carver of them and the carver of the Peacock stone.

Matthew Pittom's stone, Copp's Hill, 1693/4, is a very good illustration of this pattern, and quite aside from that has a pathetic interest, for it was put up to the memory of the son of John and Mary Pittom, who died 'aged near 20.' His father, the pewterer, had already been dead for three years and for some unexplained reason the mother chose that the boy's name should appear alone on the face of this very distinguished stone. On its back, in letters which seem to have been recut, we learn that the bodies of John and Mary also 'lie here.' Mary Pittom was grandmother of the Reverend John Comer, who records in his diary that the first thing that he remembered was 'my dear grandmother Mrs. Mary Pittom taking me into her chamber
ber

ber every evening before I went to bed and she kneeling down by the bedside caused me to do so too and used to dedicate me to the Lord. I to this day (and hope I ever shall) remember that one sentence in her prayer viz. Lord remember this child and make it thine in ye day when thou makest up thy Jewels for Christ's sake.'

This stone of Matthew Pittom has the rounded scrolls of John Cleverly, and all the Urn and Mermaid stones have an urn or vase similar to those that J. N. did; the lettering is like his, and the mermaids, instead of the streaming locks we should expect, rolled their hair in neat puffs as Deborah Thomas did.

There is also one other feature common alike to the Urns and Mermaids and to the J. N.'s. There is no epitaph, only the briefest record of death. The footstone of the Reverend Edward Tompson which bears his elegiac verse may have been carved by a different man. On the hourglass he has cut the letters J. G., perhaps his initials, so that this stone forms no exception to the sculptor's ordinary procedure. Whoever carved these stones when left to his own judgment did not care to add to the simple name and date either a bit of Latin as the old 'Stone Cutter' would have done, or a line from the Bible as Joseph Lamson, working at the same time, almost always did. To him the carving was of more importance than the inscription and above everything was the joy of creating a thing of beauty.

There is in Milford, Connecticut, a very delightful stone with a Renaissance design which suggests the work of J. N. and also of the carver of the Urns and Mermaids. It is that of Sarah Nisbett, 1698. There are many later stones in this burying-ground which were made by Massachusetts stonecutters. Many Lamsons abound both on their striped slate and on sandstone, but Sarah Nisbett's is the only specimen of fine early workmanship. The lettering is almost identical with that upon the Mermaid stone of Asaph Eliot, Granary, 1685, and we can hardly doubt that it was carved by the same hand.

Who was J. N.? No one bearing those initials is recorded in either the Suffolk or Middlesex Registry as being paid for gravestones, nor have I discovered any mason whose name commenced with these letters.

Was he John Nichols, the joiner, who lived at the North End, who
doubtless

doubtless knew all the people who ordered these stones, whose wife had many relatives in Braintree, and whose mother lived in Plymouth?

Was 'The Stone Cutter of Boston' William Dawes, the mason? His life covered the period of this man's work. When he died on March 24, 1703/4, Sewall says of him, 'A good old man, full of days, is got well to the end of his weary race.' He was eighty-five years old or 'thereabouts,' if we can rely on a deposition made by him many years previously, but, as we have seen, the work of 'The Stone Cutter' had ceased eight or ten years before. We like to think of him as a good old man.

There are many things which point to such a solution of the mystery surrounding these two early stonecutters. Some newly discovered record or some inscribed stone may at any time prove or disprove this theory.

In the meantime, they might both be satisfied to be remembered as 'The Stone Cutter of Boston' and J. N., the carver of the Peacock stone of Quincy.

CHAPTER IV
THE LAMSONS OF CHARLESTOWN

IN 1661, two worthy citizens of Ipswich petitioned the Quarterly Court of Essex County in regard to the estate of a deceased brother-in-law. William Lamson had died leaving eight young children, aged from six months to sixteen years. His widow had married again and, much to the anxiety of these thoughtful uncles, the children had been 'put out to live in other families.'

Just why we do not know. The new husband, Thomas Hartshorne, of Reading, had also eight children, and it would seem a very unfair arrangement had he kept them all while his new wife had been required to forsake hers. Probably it was not so bad as it looks. When Thomas Hartshorne died, these stepchildren called him 'my honoured father,' and, what is more significant, the boys all learned useful trades and became men of consequence in the communities where they lived.

Joseph, who was about two years old when this change came into his life, must have been a gifted child, for while his brothers gave all their time to the various businesses of being a mariner, a mason, or a bricklayer, he combined with his other occupations that of making gravestones. He was also a mariner, a cordwainer, a surveyor, but of all the descriptive titles which he could have added to his name he chose to write it, 'Joseph Lamson, Stone Cutter.' His children, grandchildren, and great-grandchildren learned his art, and Lamson gravestones were known all over New England and can be found to-day in nearly all the old burying-grounds.

Joseph Lamson was born in Ipswich in 1658, the son of William and Sarah Lamson. Whether at the time of his mother's second marriage he went with her to Reading is not known, but we find the first mention of him when a youth of eighteen he went from Mystic Side in 1675/6 with Captain Turner on the Connecticut River Expedition. Mystic Side later became Malden, and here he lived and married, in 1679, his first wife, Elizabeth Mitchell. She died in 1703, and

without

GEORGE PAYSON, DORCHESTER, 1734

SARAH BARNARD, DEERFIELD, 1720

THE FOSTER ARMS, DORCHESTER, 1732

JOHN CAPEN, DORCHESTER, 1692

without doubt he made the stone which still marks her grave in Bell Rock Burying-Ground. Her brothers were sea-captains, and at one time Joseph Lamson was one of the crew on the Thomas and Joseph, commanded by Thomas Mitchell, his brother-in-law, and probably named for its captain and his 'trusty friend,' Joseph Lamson.

We cannot doubt from the glimpses that we get of his life that he had a good business as cordwainer, but when we go into the old burying-grounds in his home town and in the towns adjacent to it, we marvel that he found time for anything outside his craft as stone-cutter. Charlestown, Malden, Revere, Woburn, Cambridge, and Watertown are so full of his work and of that of his sons, that any one of them could serve as a textbook of Lamson gravestones.

It seems evident that he learned his art from 'The Stone Cutter of Boston,' because his early stones are so similar to those which this man did that it is sometimes hard to decide which of the two made them. Both men were fond of a few words of Latin, they both used the same kind of eyebrows, and at first Lamson copied the shape of the head. It was very soon, however, that he made his work so distinctive that it is possible to distinguish it from that of all other workers. It may be that the one of the 'other families' to whom the young Joseph was 'put out' lived in Boston, where he may have served an apprenticeship, but, as far as we can learn, all his business career was spent in some part of Charlestown.

I find, in searching the Probate Records, that it is only his cheaper and poorer stones which appear in the executors' accounts. Probably when the family wished one more elaborate, they paid for it themselves, and when the decision was left to an executor or administrator, he felt as custodian of the estate that he must manage as prudently as possible.

The estate of Deacon John Hammond was settled in 1713. According to the account, Joseph Lamson was paid twenty-one shillings, probably for his gravestone, as the item immediately following reads, 'To Lamson for gravestones for the deceased's widow 0.13.0.' These stones show some of his characteristics which we are to find again and again — the drapery at the top of the stone; the little men carrying the pall; the *memento mori* and *fugit hora*, not peculiar to
him,

him, but often used by him; the heads at the top of the fruit columns; the use of small letters as well as capitals, and the narrower border of a different design across the bottom of the stone. On both these stones we see his characteristic death symbol — the broad top to the head, the highly curved eyebrows ending in almost a little hook at the outer edge, and the impassive expression.

Joseph Lamson seems to have been the first seventeenth-century stonecutter of New England to use lower-case letters as freely as the Roman capitals. 'The Stone Cutter of Boston' employed them in at least one instance for the whole inscription except the necessary capitals. This was for the stone of Joanna Ingles, Copp's Hill, 1678. Usually he considered them appropriate only for some unimportant part. Lamson, however, uses them repeatedly for almost the whole inscription, as on the stone of John Hammond. Unlike many of the early stonecutters, his capitals and spelling are always correct. He often makes his *t* a curve, as did his earlier master. Another peculiarity of his lettering is the frequent use of *th*, as in 'the,' instead of the sign '*ye*,' almost universally employed at that day. Another striking feature of his stones are the little men, also an inheritance from 'The Stone Cutter,' but after this man's death used, as far as I know, only by Joseph and for a few years by his sons. These little men were always busy doing something, carrying the pall and lowering the coffin into the grave being their usual duty, but sometimes they were holding up the hourglass for the edification of the passerby, or even more vividly bringing to his notice what would soon be his fate as they drive their darts of death into an unsuspecting skull. They always have wings, perhaps as a suggestion that heavenly creatures came to help the soul on its way to Paradise. They are apparently without clothes, except in at least one instance, on the stone of John Carter Woburn, 1692, where the extreme right-hand little man has shoe buckles.

Although in all these cases Lamson used the fruit border, he was fond of another very simple design. The account of the estate of Samuel Fletcher, Chelmsford, 1705, has an item, 'To Joseph Lamson 0.24/0,' undoubtedly for his gravestones still standing in the Chelmsford Burying-Ground.

A very

DOROTHY SPRAGUE, MALDEN, 1727

NATHANAEL NEWELL, JR., COPP'S HILL, 1717

HERE LYES BURIED
Y BODY OF
M ARTHUR MASON
AGED ABOUT
78 YEARS DEPARTED
THIS LIFE MARCH
Y 4 · 1707/8

ARTHUR MASON, GRANARY, 1707/8

CLARK ARMS, COPP'S HILL, 1743

A very finely cut and beautifully preserved specimen of Lamson's work is the stone of Peter Tufts, Malden, 1702/3. This shows many of his characteristics, and in addition he has given a moustache to each head terminating the borders. Another keystone to Joseph Lamson's work is that of Richard Kaets in Concord. The executor of Kaets's will paid Lamson for 'gravestones and carting £2.12.0.' Kaets was a mason and Boston constable. In 1712, when Sewall 'lays a rock' which he got out of the Common in the northeast corner of the foundation of the new meeting-house for the first church, he gives Kaets, who presumably did the work for him, a three-shilling bill. Kaets did not go to Concord to live until a few years before his death, but showed his interest in his new home by leaving to the church there six pounds 'to buy a silver cup for the Communion.'

In a few cases Lamson replaces the rosettes and heads at the top of his side borders with the full figure of a man, as on the stone of William Dickson, Cambridge, 1692. Here his knowledge of anatomy fails him, but not his stonecutter's skill. Notice the fine carving of the fingers and toes after two hundred and thirty-three years of New England weather.

We have seen from these stones that Joseph Lamson had no little skill in modeling faces, and sometimes he substitutes a winged head for the usual death symbol. I do not think he intended these for portraits, because he often employs an inappropriate face, as on the rather beautiful stone of John Fowle, Charlestown, 1711, where the coat-of-arms is surmounted by a curly-headed child, not by any stretch of the imagination the representation of a man 'aged 74 years.'

A very beautiful piece of work in this style is the stone of Mary Cutler, Charlestown, 1703.

Joseph Lamson did not use invariably either the borders of pomegranates and figs or the laurel leaves, but, in common with most of the stonecutters of the period, he often carved scrolls, sometimes with heads terminating the side borders and sometimes with a simple rosette, as on the stone of Deane Winthrop, Revere, 1703/4, the last son of Governor Winthrop to die, and more often recalled to mind to-day than any other member of his family because the house

where

where he lived still stands in Winthrop and the town itself bears his name.

There were other stonecutters living in Charlestown in the latter part of the seventeenth century who probably learned their trade of Joseph Lamson. Two of them, Thomas Welch and Joseph Whittemore, were cousins, the former a son of Elizabeth Upham, the latter of her sister, Mary Upham. Thomas Welch was born in 1655 and died about 1704; Joseph Whittemore was born in 1667. They also married sisters, Hannah and Joanna Mousal.

Joseph Whittemore is described by Wyman as a 'sea captain &c,' and possibly he may have brought from England or Wales some of the slate used by the Lamsons. We know him as a stonecutter only from that quaint entry of the Reverend John Baily in the church records of Watertown, especially valuable because it gives an itemized account of the price he paid for his wife's tombstone. It reads:

> For a Tombe Ston as follows;
> yr came one June 21 '92 from Connecticut, ye freight cost 8/. Carrying to the Grave from Boston, Something, for stones and lime 10/, ye Building it up was given me by Mr. Willis.
> The engraving of it cost me 12/ to Joseph Whittemore wch is but ye half of wt is usual viz. a penny a letter, he took an half penny a letter.
> For ye stone as Sett I gave £2. 5/. I payed it to Mr. John Hamlin of Middleton the fourteenth day of June 1693.

This stone for Mr. Baily's wife is still to be seen in Watertown and the letters, carved more than two hundred and thirty years ago by Joseph Whittemore, possibly recut a hundred years ago when some repairs were made, are still plainly to be read on this immense slab of Connecticut sandstone:

> Pious Lydia made and given by God
> As a most meet help to John Baily minister of the Gospel,
> Good betimes, Best at last,
> Lived by Faith, Dyed in Peace,
> Went off singing, Left us weeping,
> Walked with God until translated in the 39th year of her age April 16 1691.

The Reverend John Baily was held in high esteem, even John Dunton, who was more apt to see the curious traits in those he met than

REV. SHEARJASHUB BOURN, ROXBURY, 1768

PATIENCE WATSON, PLYMOUTH, 1767

REBECCA SANDERS, KING'S CHAPEL, 1745/6

WILLIAM SINCLAIR, SPENCER, 1753

than the more attractive ones, wrote, when he heard him preach, 'I heard Mr. John last Sunday and I thought he spoke like an angel.' Mr. Baily kept a diary, and undoubtedly, when he asked his friend, the Reverend Mr. Moody, to write an epitaph for his dear Lydia, he told him the incident recorded the day of her death in this diary:

She then desired that we would sing some psalm of praise to the riches of free grace; but our harps were hanged on the willows, we did it not. Yet there was melodious singing at that very time. I heard it myself but I intended never to speak of it until the nurse B. and M.S. spoke of it. They went into the fire thinking it was there; but they heard it best when within the curtains. God by his holy angels put an honour upon my dear little woman.

This mention by John Baily is all I have found about Joseph Whittemore's art, and not much more about Thomas Welch. There is, however, a stone standing in Billerica for which Thomas Welch was paid, that of Mary Rogers, 1697. This is almost a replica of those made by Joseph Lamson and undoubtedly the two men worked together.

Welch's inventory was taken on December 13, 1704, and includes various hammers, chisels, gouges, etc., besides a 'p'cell of working stones and building stones about the house,' suggesting that he was a builder by trade as well as a worker in the fine arts. On the succeeding February, his widow and executor makes her appearance in court as Hannah Lamson, the wife of Joseph, who thereby acquired all the above-mentioned tools and working stones, and also, as we know from the Charlestown Records of 1714, 'Thos. Welch's house ware Mr. Lamson now lives.'

This was Joseph Lamson's second marriage. Hannah Welch Lamson did not live many years as his wife, for about 1715, he married, for the third and last time, Dorothy (Hitt) Mousal.

He died August 27, 1722, in his sixty-fourth year, and his sons, Nathaniel and Caleb, were executors of his will, and charged fifty shillings for the stone which they made for him and which still leans, badly stained with smoke, in the old Phipps Street Burying-Ground in Charlestown.

Probably there were other early stonecutters in Charlestown. The
stone

stone of Hannah Killen, 1696, does not seem to be a product of Joseph Lamson's skill, and there are a number of gravestones from this period for the next twenty years which show the same bold treatment and the use of a checkerboard design, like Hannah Killen's teeth, in some part of each pattern. Lydia Wood, Charlestown, 1712, is an illustration of this checkerboard carving.

The two sons of Joseph Lamson, Nathaniel and Caleb, both stone-cutters, were destined to be as popular and as skillful as their father had been. Nathaniel was born in 1693 and Caleb in 1697. It is not easy to distinguish the work of one brother from that of the other, nor is it apparent why there should have been any preference for one over the other. But each seemed to work independently and to be paid personally for his gravestones.

From 1722 to 1767 these two brothers had almost a monopoly of their kind of business in Middlesex County as well as furnishing many stones for Boston, New Hampshire, Connecticut, and Long Island.

In the Probate Records of Middlesex and Suffolk between these dates, Nathaniel Lamson was paid by at least forty-six adminis-trators or executors, Caleb by fifty-four and 'Mr. Lamson of Charlestown' by forty-nine. It is hard to say what proportion of accounts mention gravestones, perhaps one in thirty or forty, and not more than half of those give the name of the stonecutter. 'Paid for gravestones' is usually the brief entry; from which we judge that these hundred and fifty represent many hundreds.

I have never found a stone made by Joseph Lamson upon which he carved his initials, but occasionally both Nathaniel and Caleb signed their work. This was especially true in their early days. One which Nathaniel has so signed is that of Mrs. Mary Rous, Charles-town, 1714/5. This is very delicately and beautifully carved, and it is quite possible that it was done by the father, who turned it over to Nathaniel for an inscription. Captain William Rous could well afford such a fine stone for his wife, for not long before he had come home in the Sapphire, bringing with him his Spanish prize which had on board a considerable quantity of Spanish milled dollars and silks. He was the son of parents bearing the remarkable names of Faithful and Suretrust Rous.   Another

WILLIAM MOORE, GRANARY, 1761

SETH SUMNER, MILTON, 1771

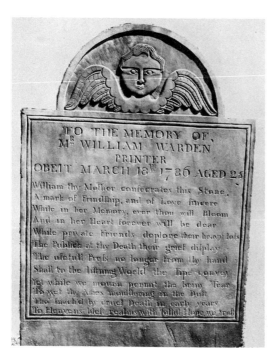

TO THE MEMORY OF,
Mr WILLIAM WARDEN
PRINTER
OBEIT MARCH 18th 1786 AGED 25

William thy Mother consecrates this Stone,
A mark of Frindſhip, and of Love ſincere
While in her Memory, ever thou will Bloom
And in her Heart forever will be dear
While private Friends deplore their heavy loſs
The Publick at thy Death their grief diſplay
The uſefull Preſs no longer from thy hand
Shall to the liſtning World the line convey
Yet while we mourn permit the briny Tear
To wet thy Aſhes mouldering in the Duſt
Tho ſnatch'd by cruel Death in early years
To Heavens bleſt realms with fond Hope we truſt

WILLIAM WARDEN, GRANARY, 1786

Here lies buried
the Body of
Mrs ANN MALCOM
Widow of
Capt DANIEL MALCOM
died April 4th 1770.
Aged 40 Years.

ANN MALCOLM, COPP'S HILL, 1770

Another stone bearing the initials N. L. is that of the Reverend Jonathan Pierpont, Wakefield, who died in 1709 when Nathaniel was only sixteen years old. It may not have been erected for some years after that date, or it may again have been the father's work with the inscription carved by Nathaniel. It is a beautiful stone and beautifully cut. Nothing was considered too good for the Reverend Jonathan — 'the painful, faithful useful and humble minister of Reading,' as Cotton Mather calls him. All the ministers and all his friends seemed to agree that he was a very great loss and merited all that is carved on his gravestone:

> A Fruitful Christian, And a pastor who
> Did good to all and lov'd all good to do,
> A tender Husband and a parent Kind
> A Faithful Friend which who oh who can find
> A Preacher that a bright example gave
> Of Rules he preached the souls of Men to save.
> A Pierpont all of this here leaves his dust
> And waits the Resurrection of the Just.

A stone very similar to this is one made for Captain and Mrs. Pyam Blower. She died in Cambridge May 29, 1709, and he June 1, just one day before the Reverend Jonathan Pierpont. The little ministers with their Bibles clasped to their breasts are replaced by a man with folded hands wearing a wig on the Captain's side and a woman with hair in puffs and a laced bodice on hers.

Among the stones signed by Caleb there are none so beautiful as those on which Nathaniel carved his initials. Among them those of Mary Reed, 1712/3, and Prudence Turner, 1717, are in Marblehead. In both these cases 'her' is spelled 'har,' a mistake Joseph would not have made.

Very soon, however, we can easily distinguish the work of these two brothers from that of their father, although they continued to use the fruit and scroll designs which he had employed. They very early adopted a distinctive device. Whether this was intended for some modification of the fig or whether it was an arbitrary conventional figure, it is not easy to determine. We find its beginnings sometimes in the father's work, but the sons made it their own. It

appears

appears several times on the stone of Mary Robinson, Duxbury, 1722, that young girl who 'perished in the Mighty Deep' with her mother, an accident which sent a thrill of horror over New England and was the occasion of sermons and poems as well as of two gravestones. This one of the daughter still stands in Duxbury. The mother's body was washed ashore at Provincetown and the stone which marked her resting-place, they tell me, is gone. It had an inscription written by her husband, the Reverend John Robinson, which closed with the quotation from the Psalms, 'Thus he bringeth them to their desired haven.'

The Lamsons sometimes combined this device with the scroll, as on the stone of Jonathan Remington, Cambridge, 1738, a stone which shows very clearly the striped slate often used by them. This is in various delicate colors, blue, red, green, and ochre, often with the stripes running diagonally, as on the stone of Mrs. Hepsibah Prentice, Cambridge, 1741/2, a stone, by the way, which conclusively proves that Paige, the 'Prentice Genealogy,' and all the genealogists since their day were wrong when they gave Solomon Prentice two wives, the first being Elizabeth. Had Hepsibah been obliged to give up to this mythical Elizabeth her oldest son Solomon, she never could have had written on her gravestone, 'thair had Desended From her 140 Persons.'

The Lamsons also used a footstone which can be seen by the hundreds in the old burying-grounds, always carrying their device, sometimes with a border, sometimes without.

In the Phipps Street Burying-Ground at Charlestown, there is a row of tombs closed by large slabs of slate upon which are engraved coats-of-arms. It is probable that most of these were carved by the Lamsons. The slate has the diagonal stripes which are seen so often on their gravestones, and many of them date from the time when Nathaniel and Caleb were doing their best work.

With the death of Nathaniel in 1755 and of Caleb in 1769, the most interesting work of the Lamson family came to an end. Nathaniel's son Joseph and Caleb's son John were also stonecutters and makers of gravestones. Apparently they were men of little originality and in trying to adjust the designs of their fathers to the taste of the day,
they

they made lightly cut stones of no especial merit or interest. One of the best which I have discovered done by one of the third generation of Lamsons is that of Mrs. Abigail Codman, Haverhill, 1775.

One Lamson at least of the next generation carried on the family employment, Joseph, son of Joseph, born in 1760. He died in 1808, when the wonderful career of the Lamson family as carvers of gravestones came to an end. From 1658, when the first Joseph was born, until 1808, when the last Joseph died, their lives had covered a century and a half.

CHAPTER V
THE FOSTERS OF DORCHESTER

THE ancient burying-ground in Dorchester has on the whole received good care. Inside the high walls surrounding the Old North, there are fifty-seven seventeenth-century stones, besides six equally early tombs. When William Blake made his will in 1661, he gave 'unto the Town of Dorchester twenty shillings to be bestowed for ye repairing of ye Burying Place so yt swine and other vermine may not anoy ye graves of ye saints.'

From that time until the middle of the nineteenth century, there are many items in the Town Records relating to its care. As late as 1838, the Town removed twelve cartloads of brambles out of the center of the burying-ground, which also was 'full of Holes and Snakes.'

There is only one of 'the graves of ye saints' which is now marked with a stone that antedates the making of William Blake's will — that of Bernard Capen and his wife, 1653, and what was left of their gravestone was removed some years ago to the library of the New England Historic Genealogical Society and one in a much later style substituted for it.

There are a few so-called 'wolf stones,' rough and flat, covering the whole surface of several unnamed graves — the heavy stones put down as a guard, not against wolves alone, but even more the 'other vermine' which frequented the spot. There are also two tombs of only a few months' later date than the will. Before, however, 'the Relicts of William Blake' paid over eighteen shillings of the legacy in 1668, one other, Steven Minot, had been buried. Probably William Blake's money was instrumental in saving many of the stones erected between 1670 and 1700.

A large majority of these early stones have no ornamentation. They are carefully, sometimes beautifully, lettered. Many of them have been recut. We do, however, find some which without hesitation we can assign to 'The Stone Cutter of Boston.' Very early we meet

JOHN COLEMAN, GRANARY, 1771

JOHN ELIOT FOOTSTONE, GRANARY, 1771

REV. SAMUEL RUGGLES, BILLERICA, 1737

PAUL TITCOMB, NEWBURYPORT, 1773

meet with others done by the Fosters in a distinctive style of their own, and while they were working — until 1772 — the Dorchester people rarely patronized any other stonecarver.

James Foster, Gentleman, of Dorchester, is the only early stone-cutter of whom we know even approximately the figure and linea-ments. As we study his gravestone, made possibly by himself or more probably by his son James, we can imagine that he was a rather handsome, well-dressed man, perhaps with wider shoulders than the oval of the design permitted, dignified and carrying off exceedingly well the primly curled wig and the scarf and ruffled shirt. By his side is buried his first wife, Priscilla, whose stone undoubtedly was done by him and probably intended to portray her features. We find on it some of the characteristics which we shall recognize later as pe-culiar to him, a certain definiteness of line, as if he always kept his tools well-sharpened, a broad, flat manner of portraying scrolls, and deeply incised rosettes. Priscilla's chin, too, rests on a support below as usually do the chins of his cherubs.

On his right hand lie his parents, James and Anna, and on their stone is beautifully carved the Foster arms, with the same flat, sharply cut scrolls and deeply incised rosettes, and the tablets bear-ing the inscriptions are in the shape of a heart, as is Priscilla's, and the lettering also is similar to hers.

We can scarcely doubt that the same hand carved the rather beau-tiful coat-of-arms on the back of the stone of the Reverend Andrew Eliot, Copp's Hill, which together with the tomb was bought by the heirs of the Reverend Andrew from 'Mrs. Watts' about 1770. They paid John Homer £2.30. 'for altering the stone,' the alteration con-sisting in turning this fine piece of work to the wall, and preparing what had been the back for an inscription when it should be needed for the Reverend Andrew. He must have been a well-loved minister, for the Reverend Caleb Gannett wrote in his Almanac, 'It was a pleasant day Sept. 15 1778 when near four hundred couples and thirty-two carriages followed the remains of Rev. Andrew Eliot from his house before the south side of his meeting house' — he was the pastor of the North Church, and his house still stands on the corner of Hanover and Tileston Streets — 'in to Fore St. up Cross St.
through

through Black Horse Lane to Corpse Hill.' If there were four in each carriage there would have been about nine hundred and twenty-eight persons in this funeral procession.

There were three James Fosters in Dorchester — James of the portrait stone, his father, and his son.

In the Probate Records of Middlesex and Suffolk I have found over one hundred instances where some Foster, usually James, sometimes Mr. or Captain, was paid by estates, in the majority of cases for gravestones. The earliest payment is for the stone of Hannah Ware, 1722, and the latest a group purchased from the widow of the third James, soon after his death in 1771.

We can be very sure that the second and third James made gravestones, and it seems almost as certain that the first one also did.

The first James Foster was the son of Hopestill and Mary (Bates) Foster, born in 1651; married, first, Mary, the daughter of John Capen; second, Anna, daughter of Job Lane, of Malden. He died in 1732. He might very well have been engraving stones as late as 1722, the date of Hannah Ware's gravestone, for which a James Foster was paid. The strongest reason, however, for concluding that the first James was also a stonecutter is the fact that there are many stones bearing all the marks of the Foster hand which are much too early to have been done by the second James. Both fathers-in-law to the first James have Foster stones — John Capen in Dorchester, 1692, and Job Lane in Malden, 1697. That of Job Lane is in quite a different style from those we have previously seen, but the death's-head is the Foster death's-head, and rests its square jaw on the tablet below in the real Foster attitude. Thankful Baker, a sister of the first James, has a very similar stone, and we find this design of a little vine used many times in the seventeenth century. It was especially popular for children's stones and does not seem to have been confined to the Fosters. When wrought neatly and carefully, it probably was their work, while the many poorer carvings in this or a similar pattern may have been done by a less careful stonecutter.

Another design often used in one form or another by the early Fosters is that on the stone of little Joseph Nightingale, Quincy, 1715. We can easily recognize the Foster death's-head, but the work

seems

TOBIAS LEAR, PORTSMOUTH, N. H., 1781

JOHN HURD, GRANARY, 1784

JOHN HOLYOKE, NEWTON, 1775

REV. NATHANIEL ROGERS, IPSWICH, 1775

seems like drawing on a child's slate, which could easily be rubbed off with a damp sponge; yet it has stood through all the mists and fogs and rains of two hundred years unchanged. The same design is on the stone of Joseph Barnard, Deerfield, 1695; on that of Benjamin Thompson, 'the learned schoolmaster,' Roxbury, 1714; and in high-relief on that of James Trott, Dorchester, 1719, as well as on many others.

I think it is safe to say that all these very early stones were carved by the first James. There was much talent in the Foster family and they all seemed to do some kind of handiwork. This James was a younger brother of John, the talented engraver and printer; another brother was a gunsmith, and a third a goldsmith. From the fact that James did not make the stone for his brother John and that we find none in his style before the nineties, I think we can say that he did not take up the business of being a stonecutter until after John's death in 1681.

The most interesting work of this first James was his very original and complicated scrolls. These we see on the stone of his father-in-law, John Capen, 1692, and from that period through the first two decades of the eighteenth century they are very abundant. The second James followed so closely in his father's footsteps that it is not possible to differentiate their work. The fine stones in Weston for Benoni Garfield and his wife, for which James Foster, Jr., received five pounds in 1727, have the same kind of intricate scrolls as does John Capen's, thirty-five years earlier. As far as I have discovered, the Fosters never exactly repeated their patterns except in the very simplest of them all.

The same year, 1727, James Foster was paid two pounds for the gravestone of Dorothy Sprague, of Malden. The father at this time was seventy-six, and we imagine that he was not doing much stone-cutting, but doubtless turned over his slate, his tools, and his designs to his son.

This second James was the son of the first James and his second wife, Anna Lane. He was born December 8, 1698, married, first, Priscilla, secondly, Mrs. Elizabeth Pimer, and died January 8, 1763, sixty-five years old.

Either

Either the father or the son may have made the stone of Stephen Williams, Roxbury, 1720. I should guess, however, that it was the younger man who dared to inaugurate a radical change in the well-established death symbol, by placing eyeballs in the empty sockets. It gives you a curious feeling, accustomed as you are to these hollow-eyed, impassive heads, to catch sight of one which is looking at you with a semblance of life and interest. The pine cones, too, make a unique border, used, as far as I have discovered, only by the Fosters.

The second James did not continue to make the elaborate scrolls or the delicate engravings many years after his father's death. A simpler, heavier style came into vogue. In 1736 he was paid eighty shillings for the gravestone of George Payson, Dorchester, a very fair example of his later work.

As his father's work had overlapped his by eight or ten years, so his overlapped his son's. The third James, son of his first wife, Priscilla, was born March 3, 1732, and to add to the confusion of the records, he, too, was a captain. He married, July 7, 1754, Mary Robinson. His work can be distinguished from that of his father and grandfather, but on the whole it is not especially interesting. Several of the stones for which he was paid are still standing in Dorchester, one for Eunice Clapp, one for Eleanor Shippey, and a third, with the same pear-shaped face and blank expression, for his stepmother, Elizabeth. He showed some initiative in returning to the old symbols, long discarded in his day, the hourglass, the cross-bones, the pickaxe, and the spade. He died June 4, 1771, and left a large estate, probably much of it received from his father, who after a common fashion of those days divided his property without taking the trouble to go through the Probate Court. His stonecutter's tools were valued at over nine pounds and the slate stone on the place was twenty-seven pounds. He had a negro boy and a good array of farm animals.

The Foster farm was on Dorchester Neck, in that part which later became South Boston. The mansion house, 'the most elegantly furnished house on the Neck,' was destroyed by the British in 1776.

I have found no mention, either in the Town Records, deeds, or private papers, that any one of these three men was a stonecutter. Only the Probate Registries of Suffolk and Middlesex Counties,

hidden

hidden away in their dusty old books, have kept this information. Dorchester is full of their work. Roxbury and Milton have nearly as much. Boston, on the contrary, has very little — she had stone-cutters enough of her own; but other towns, Brookline, Quincy, and Portsmouth, New Hampshire, have each a few.

There is one other member of the family who may have been a maker of gravestones, Hopestill, the brother of the second James. He was born in 1771, married, in 1724, Sarah Allen, and died in 1772. He is called a housewright, but once, in 1749, there is an entry in the Suffolk Records in the settlement of the estate of William Bullard, Jr., 'Pd Hopestill Foster for Gravestones £5.' It is a characteristic Foster stone and may have been done by him or possibly he was act-ing as agent for his brother. His inventory shows a goodly array of hammers and chisels, gouges and wedges, all useful to either a house-wright or a stonecutter.

The Fosters had a kinsman who seems to have been very helpful in placing orders for them. Ebenezer Barnard was a clothier, the son of Joseph Barnard, of Northampton. For a few years in his early life he lived in Roxbury, and married Elizabeth, the daughter of the first of the three James Fosters. While he was there we find in two in-stances, about 1722, that Mr. Barnard was paid for gravestones. Both of these stones are still in the Eustis Street Burying-Ground, and both without much doubt are Foster stones. Before this time the Fosters — at least the first James — had worked for Deerfield patrons, and the oldest stone now remaining in the burying-ground there was from his hand and for a Joseph Barnard, who died in 1695. Another, a very fine and very characteristic piece of Foster work, is one for Sarah Barnard, who died in 1720, both these stones suggesting some connection between the Fosters and the Barnards earlier than the time when Ebenezer Barnard married Elizabeth Foster.

CHAPTER VI

THE EIGHTEENTH-CENTURY STONECUTTERS OF BOSTON

WITH the coming of the eighteenth century, there came many new carvers of gravestones. As long as William Mumford lived, his work seems to have been preferred to that of the younger men. In the first few years of the new century, J. N. produced his most notable stones, but we find little that we can ascribe to his skillful hand after 1705.

The new men had learned their art from this older generation, but with the sureness of youth, they chose other designs and other methods of expression. Looking back at them from this long distance of time, they do not seem so fine, but evidently they pleased their own generation, and from their numbers we can select a few who were easily the most popular and most successful gravestone-makers of their day.

These were Nathaniel Emmes, William Codner, Henry Christian Geyer, John Homer, and, towards the end of the century, Daniel Hastings, of Newton. All left sons who were stonecutters.

One Scotchman, who died in 1722 when only thirty-three years old, was paid for several stones in his short career, and undoubtedly had he lived would have been equally popular with these others. His name was James Gilchrist and he is buried in King's Chapel. I have found no stone now standing for which he was paid, but three which are rather similar to each other, signed 'J. G.,' were probably from his hand. One is in Copp's Hill, that of Thomas Killon, 1708, and the other two, a small one for Mary Green, 1709, and another for John Macintoshe, 1710, are in the Granary.

There was another Boston man working at the same time whose initials were also J. G., John Gaud. As far as I know only one of the few stones for which he was paid is in existence, that of Samuel Holbrook, Granary, 1721. There are many like it, and probably John Gaud was responsible for them all, but they do not seem to be the work of the J. G. who signed the others. There is, however, at Copp's

Hill

ANNA BARNARD, MARBLEHEAD, 1774

SAMUEL ROCKWOOD, GROTON, 1753

SUSANNA HILL, BILLERICA, 1758

MERCY DABY, GROTON, 1751

Hill a large triple stone which may have been his work — that of the tragic Worthylakes, the lighthouse keeper who, with his wife and daughter, Ruth, was drowned when coming over to Boston from Noddle's Island in 1718. Cotton Mather preached a sermon and Benjamin Franklin, a youth at that time, wrote a poem about them which was sold as a broadside on the street. Just a month and a day after this occurrence, John Gaud married the daughter, Anne Worthylake, and became administrator of the father's estate. He paid £4.10.0. for their gravestone, possibly to himself.

NATHANIEL EMMES

In 1691, Judge Sewall sends to England for some wrought stones for 'coins' for his house. It was two years before he received them, and then they were not to his mind. He writes, 'The costliness of them bespeaks a Grandeur far beyond my estate which I have purposely avoided; which was one reason made me forbid sending for silk, out of a particular dislike I had to the wearing so much in this poor country.'

Perhaps this was also the reason that the thoughtful Judge never had a coach of his own and why sometimes, when he wished to ride farther than he liked to ask his horse to carry his two hundred and twenty-eight pounds, he would hire 'Em's his coach.' The owner of this coach was Henry Emmes, constable in 1685, messenger to the General Court in 1694, a baker — a respectable and useful member of the community. He probably lived on Prince Street, as later did his son, Nathaniel, and the boy Nathaniel must have known every nook and corner of William Mumford's workshop. That he learned the art of making gravestones from this near neighbor we can hardly doubt. Born in 1690, he was twenty-eight years old when William Mumford died. The first time when he is recorded as being paid for a gravestone was in 1717, the year before Mumford's death. Probably his hand had helped out in many of the older man's stones, but new styles were coming in. The beautiful borders of flowers and fruit were not quite the thing and their carving took too much time. The new generation preferred bolder effects, something less archaic, and Nathaniel Emmes catered to this demand. Perhaps to make his
work

work distinctive and perhaps because he struck a good bargain, he discarded the fine blue stone which William Mumford had used and chose to work almost exclusively on a reddish slate. It has not stood the test of time so well, often splitting badly, but because of its use we can easily select Emmes's work in the old burying-grounds. Later he, too, preferred the blue slate. In 1718 he was paid £1.10.0. by the estate of Nathanael Newell, undoubtedly for the stone which still stands in Copp's Hill, with its hollow eyes, heavy scroll, narrow border at bottom and over the curve of the top — all characteristics of much of his later work.

There is a gravestone in the Granary which has the letters 'N. E.' cut at the top. It is shaped from a rough black slate badly broken and carelessly done, but in some way suggesting the rugged character of the man it commemorates, Arthur Mason, of whom John Dunton writes, 'a grave sober merchant, a good man and well respected, amongst honest men downright honest but very blunt.' He was a baker with a warehouse near the Common. He died in 1708 when Emmes was only eighteen, and this rough carving must have been among his earliest attempts.

From 1717 to 1753 I have found eighty-seven estates which paid Nathaniel Emmes either specifically for gravestones or amounts which were probably for them. Like nearly all the early stonecutters his business life included many activities besides the carving of gravestones. One of the most important of these other employments was laying the foundations for buildings. Among the crowds hurrying down Milk Street every day, the hundredth man is arrested by the letters clearly cut on the cornerstone of the Old South Church, 'N.E. March 31 1729,' and perhaps he gives a moment's thought to the man who placed them there. On another stone on the northwestern corner are the initials 'I.B. 1729,' those of Joshua Blanchard, who wrote in his diary, '1729 April ye 1st. I with other layd the foundation of the south Brick meeting house and finished the brick work ye 8th. of October following.' Joshua Blanchard was a bricklayer and builder, Nathaniel Emmes the most important stonecutter in Boston in 1729. It would seem very probable that he was the 'other' who helped Blanchard lay the foundations of the church, the 'N.E.' of the cornerstone.   As

MARY BUCKMAN, LEXINGTON, 1768

SARAH BALDWIN, BILLERICA, 1761

JUDAH MONIS, NORTHBOROUGH, 1764

JAMES BARRETT, CONCORD, 1778

As Emmes grew older, the character of his work underwent a change, his bold scrolls and rather careless effects giving place to more conventional, neater borders, and less expressive death symbols. Apparently he did his work for the money that was in it rather than for any very deep artistic feeling, and when he died on April 7, 1750, he left a mansion house on Prince Street, a parcel of stones and slate worth forty pounds, another house with land on Middle Street, and to his wife, in addition to her third of his estate, his 'negro woman named Phillis absolutly forever.' This property, however, was not so great as it seems, for his houses and lands were mortgaged.

His two sons, Joshua and Henry, went on with his business, their work being much like that done by their father in his later years.

WILLIAM CODNER

As Emmes seems to have learned his art of William Mumford, so William Codner was apparently a pupil of Emmes, having, however, the originality and imagination which the latter lacked. William Codner was the son of James, a cooper, living on Cross Street, very near the houses of Mumford and Emmes. He was born July 24, 1709, and when his father died in 1738, Nathaniel Emmes was one of his appraisers. Mary Giles, a niece of William Codner, married Henry Emmes, son of Nathaniel, so socially the families were closely connected, and undoubtedly equally close business relations account for the fact that the ordinary, what we might call the hackwork, of Nathaniel Emmes and of William Codner is so very much alike that it is impossible to distinguish the work of one man from that of the other.

William Codner married Mary Hill, of Cambridge, thereby becoming brother-in-law to three ministers and uncle to a governor, Governor Eustis, of Massachusetts. His wife outlived him many years, spending the last years of her life in Stockbridge.

From 1731 to 1764, Codner was paid by at least seventy-five estates, but, as is usual in these Probate Records, most of these stones are in his rather poorer and more conventional style. But one of them is among his very best, the beautiful coat-of-arms made in 1743 for William Clark. He received forty pounds for his share of the work, while Thomas Johnson, the artist, was paid for escutcheons and the
                                                                          drawing

drawing of the arms which Codner copied fifty-seven pounds, ninety-seven pounds in all — a goodly sum in those days to be expended by a family who were left 'not very rich' as Hannah Mather Crocker tells us. William Clark had been very rich and had built himself a mansion which has been called 'a monument of human pride.' He was a merchant and shipowner. One by one his fleet of forty ships had been destroyed in the French wars, and Mrs. Crocker says it was a 'broken spirited man' whose mortal part was laid away under these beautifully carved arms. The picture of his three-story brick house, with its high-boy entrance and twenty-five windows on the front, is very familiar to us, but it is not now remembered by the name of its first owner. After William Clark's death, when there was little money left for the family, it was sold to Sir Harry Frankland and later became the home of his widow, Agnes Surriage. Still later it was occupied by the Webster family, whose son, John White Webster, was principal in that very tragic Parkman murder. It also figures as the residence of Mrs. Lechmere in 'Lionel Lincoln.'

No wonder these more romantic and tragic associations completely obscured the history of the 'eminent merchant' and 'honourable counsellor' who built the house and who had his coat-of-arms inlaid in the middle of the parlor floor, and also had 'mantels exquisitely carved in imitation of fruit and flowers.'

The Clark family were not finicky about the delineation of their coat-of-arms if we can believe the description of the inlay of the parlor floor, which does not correspond very closely with the drawing made by Thomas Johnson which William Codner followed on the tombstone. Both have swans, one on the shield and the other on the crest, and rather curiously the swan is a type of patience and Christian resignation, because the swan sings when it is about to die, an attribute which William Clark must have needed. It was not enough that his property should be swept away and his house known by the name of another; he was not allowed to rest in peace on the narrow bit of land he had chosen on Copp's Hill. One Samuel Winslow, a Boston sexton, appropriated it, and it is known to-day as the Winslow tomb.

Thomas Johnson may have added the garlands of fruits and flowers

THOMAS BARRETT, CONCORD, 1779

JOSIAH BURGE, WESTFORD, 1756

JOSEPH WHEELER, NORTHBOROUGH, 1747

JONAS GALE, HOLDEN, 1784

ers to his drawing or they may have been the choice of William Codner, inspired, perhaps, in either case by the flowers and fruit of the
Clark mantels. They proved to be a lasting inspiration to William
Codner as many of his later stones show. Rebecca Sanders, King's
Chapel, 1745/6, has a very similar border, and in addition Time and
Death having their usual struggle over the extinguishment of Rebecca's candle of life, a very favorite design of Codner's. On this
stone, as on many others, he shows a greater knowledge of anatomy
than many of his contemporaries. The skeleton representing death
strikes a natural attitude, well-braced for the work in hand. In fact
we can say that William Codner almost always makes his skeletons
quite at home and comfortable whatever they are doing, with bright
eyes and a good set of lower as well as upper teeth.

In the country churchyard of Spencer, there is one stone which
stands out from the others as being wrought by a master hand. It is
that of William Sinclair, 1753. It is of smooth blue slate, while
almost all around it are made from splintery, iron-rusty schist. Who
but William Codner would carve so comfortable a skeleton and put a
pillow under his head?

There are many stones in Plymouth probably made by him, the
little borders of grapes, pears, and corn furnishing the clue, a few
comfortable skeletons, and many portraits. His portrait work appears in the virile cherub on the stone of the Reverend Shearjashub
Bourne, who is buried in Roxbury, but who was from the Cape. For
this stone he was paid in 1768 four pounds. Among others in Plymouth which seem to be his work is that of Patience Watson with
her little pointed waist and gold locket, suggesting an old-time min-
iature.

William Codner died September 12, 1769, sixty years old. His
sons, Abraham and John, made a few gravestones for Boston patrons,
but John died soon after his father and Abraham removed to Stockbridge, where his sister Mary was living, the wife of the Reverend
John Sargent. The other two sons were both Tories and left Boston
for more loyal climes, William, the oldest, to live and die in London,
James, the youngest, in St. John's, New Brunswick. It may be they
followed their father's trade in these places where they dwelt.

Henry

HENRY CHRISTIAN GEYER

The third Boston stonecutter of the eighteenth century to attain a widespread reputation was Henry Christian Geyer. Judging from the names in his family he was of German ancestry. Most of what we know about them, we glean from his grandmother's will. She was Anna Maria Geyer, and she remembers, by name, not only her own children, but also her grandchildren, including Henry Christian Geyer, son of her son, George Ludovick Geyer, and his wife, Phillipin. The family lived in that part of Boston called the South End.

In 1773, Peter Geyer and Henry C. Geyer were both members of John Haskin's company of militia and both are described as fishermen. Both served in the Revolution, Peter, the uncle, being commander of the privateer, Fair Trader. Just how Henry Christian divided his time between his nets and chisels is not apparent, but, judging from the large number of gravestones made by him and still remaining in many a New England burying-ground, stonecutting was his real vocation. Probably like all fishermen, the day's result was of small consequence to him, and perhaps it was on the banks of the Charles or floating down Boston Harbor that the ideas came to him for his most daring designs. Certainly the cutting of an ordinary gravestone had got to be a rather monotonous and dull art in Boston by the middle of the eighteenth century, William Codner being the only stonecutter who was putting into his work either thought or imagination, and Henry Christian Geyer burst upon the town with originality and genuine vivacity.

He married, in 1757, Thankful Bolter, daughter of Cornelius, the baker, who deeded to him a piece of land fronting on Frog Lane as Boylston Street was then called, and apparently not far from the corner of Washington Street.

Henry Christian was a good advertiser, a booster for home-made goods and his own wares, an exceedingly up-to-date man, one who we feel sure, should he return to his old haunts, would instantly be elected to membership in Rotary and prove himself a good member and an all-round good fellow.

The stone of William Moore, Granary, 1761, is one of the earliest for which there is a record of his being paid. He received for this

£1.8.0.

ANN CUNNINGHAM, SPENCER, 1775

JOSHUA NICHOLS, BROOKFIELD, 1759

MARY MOORE, OXFORD, 1761

ROBERT CUTLER, BROOKFIELD, 1760

£1.8.0. It has some of his most characteristic features, the crown, which he uses over and over again, the little winged heads at an unusual angle, and especially the figures in the middle of each border, the parallelograms filled in in this case with curved lines, but oftener left without. John Eliot's stone, 1771, not far from this in the Granary, is quite similar, but from the footstone we get an entirely different style of Geyer's work, and see the way he catered to simple tastes and flat wallets. Although on his larger, better stones he preferred cherubs' heads with wings and hair, when he did make a death's-head, this was the way he did it.

His masterpiece in originality, the gravestone of Mrs. Susanna Jayne, Marblehead, 1776, has a representation of death with the same kind of nose, eyes, and teeth. This, however, has so much of a symbolic nature that it will be left for a later chapter.

By 1760, Geyer was advertising in the 'Boston Newsletter,' from his shop near the South Fish Market. At first he quite ignores the women and 'informs his customers and all other gentlemen.' By 1767, he describes his location as being near the Tree of Liberty, and, besides his usual work in slate and sandstone, he advertises, 'Stone coverts which may be erected in any convenient place on a Gentleman's house, in order to preserve any sort of provision or Liquor from spoiling and are very convenient for Gentlewomen' — his first reference to women — 'to preserve their milk, cream and cold Victuals,' a kind of forerunner of our refrigerators.

However, he reaches the climax of his advertising in 1770, on January 25, when he has the following card in the 'Newsletter':

HENRY CHRISTIAN GEYER
Stone cutter near Liberty Tree
South Boston

Hereby informs his Customers and other Gentlemen and Ladies that besides carrying on the Stone Cutting business as usual he carries on the Art and Manufactory of a Sister Simolacrocum, or the making of all sorts of Images viz: — 1st. Kings and Queens, 2nd. King George and Queen Charlotte, 3rd. King and Queen of Prussia, 4th. King and Queen of Denmark, 5th. King and Queen of Sweden, Likewise a number of busts, among which are Matthew Prior, Homer, Milton &c. also a number of animals such as Parrots, Cats, Dogs, Lions, Sheep with a number of others too many to
enumerate,

enumerate, — Said Geyer also cleans old deficient Animals and makes them look as well as new at a reasonable rate. All the above mentioned Images, Animals &c. are made of Plaister of Paris of this Country Produce and man- ufactured at a reasonable rate by said Geyer who cleans Ments and polishes marble of all sorts. —

Inasmuch as said Geyer has been at a considerable Expense within these four years in making Preparations in order to accomplish said Manufactory he hopes the Gentlemen and Ladies will be so kind as to favour him with their Custom and they may depend on being well used.

N.B. Any Merchants, Masters of Vessels, County Traders, Shopkeepers &c. may be supplied with what quantity they may have occasion for by giving timely notice to said Geyer.

Perhaps his great fondness for crowns came from his ability to make pleasing kings and queens.

In one case, at least, he seems to have attempted portraiture. John Coleman, who was buried in the Granary in 1771, with his straight nose, upward-curving lips, and carelessly rumpled hair, seems quite like a real person. He has a full quota of masonic em- blems — a very early instance of their use on a gravestone.

Very rarely Geyer signs a stone, as he did that of Mr. Seth Sum- ner, Milton, 1771. On this we have not only the two heads and the crown, but the sun, moon, and the seven stars of the Pleiades, the new Heaven and the new Earth of the Revelation. The seven stars, as we learn from Saint John, were the Angels of the Seven Churches, and all who had been shining lights in this world were confidently expected to shine as the stars forever and ever in the next.

I have not learned when he died, but when Anna Maria Geyer, the grandmother, made her will in 1791, she devises to 'John Just Geyer, son of my grandson, Henry Christian Geyer dec'd,' probably his only child living at that time.

John Just Geyer inherited his estate and went on with his business. His level-eyed cherubs bear a family resemblance to the rather livelier ones his father used to cut, and his work is very much in evidence in the burying-grounds of Boston and neighboring towns.

A typical specimen is the neatly cut stone of William Warden, 1786, which has the distinction of having the longest poem engraved upon it of all the gravestones in the Granary.

                                                                        As

ROBERT GODDARD, MILLBURY, 1786

REV. DAVID THURSTON, AUBURN, 1777

JOHN GRAHAM, SPENCER, 1776

SARAH MOORE, BROOKFIELD, 1761

As far as I know, no stone marks the grave of either of the Geyers. They are remembered only by the work they did for others.

JOHN HOMER

Contemporaneous with Emmes, Codner, and Geyer was Captain John Homer. He may have been the John Homer, son of John and Anne (Mortar) Homer, born in Boston December 23, 1727, married Abigail, and had Abigail in 1753 and John in 1755. We know later that he had a son William in business with him, but on the whole the Boston Records throw very little light on his family.

September 30, 1769, John Rowe writes in his diary, 'This day the Custom House officers made a large seizure from Captain John Homer who I take to be a very honest good man and for which I am very sorry should happen at this time.' He does not tell us the character of this seizure, but only a year before, Homer's friend, the merchant Daniel Malcolm, had smuggled in at night a cargo of sixty casks of wine from a vessel anchored down the harbor. This act and doubtless that of Captain Homer were to express their hatred of the injustice of the revenue acts, for both men were prominent in the activities which a few years later precipitated the Revolution. Only the previous month we find the Captain dining with other Sons of Liberty at the Liberty Tree at Dorchester. Probably to-day John Homer's name is oftenest read on the wonderful silver bowl made for the 'Fifteen Associates' to the memory of the glorious ninety-two members of the House of Representatives of Massachusetts Bay who voted 'not to rescind.' This Assembly had been asked by Governor Bernard to rescind a vote they had passed in 1767 to raise a committee of correspondence, a move considered by the King and Ministry of England as exceedingly dangerous.

The 'Fifteen Associates' who ordered this immense bowl of Paul Revere were a body of men calling themselves 'The Union Club,' mostly mechanics, but at their secret meetings planning the measures which should be undertaken to bring about the desired liberty. The bowl now is in the Metropolitan Art Museum inscribed with the names of this dauntless Fifteen. Besides John Homer's we read that of Daniel Malcolm, the merchant of Fleet Street, who died October 23, 1769, possibly before Paul Revere had finished the bowl.

A true

A true son of Liberty
A Friend to the Publick
An Enemy to Oppression
And one of the foremost
in opposing the Revenue Acts
of America.

Captain John Homer sorrowfully made his gravestone and in May, 1770, he was paid for a similar one for his wife, Ann, £2. 13. 4. Both of these stones survived their rough treatment by the soldiers of the King, who, after reading the epitaph on Daniel's stone, felt themselves particularly justified in using them both as targets and joking about the big black eye they gave to Ann. But her nose remains as John Homer made it. More conventional and correct was his usual skull and cross-bones, like that of Paul Titcomb, Newburyport, 1773.

From 1758 to 1797 he was paid for about forty stones and, as far as I have found them, these forty were ornamented with this favorite design. If he did all that were done in this style, and I have not found one of that period or locality attributed to any other stonecutter, there must be hundreds which he made still in existence. Among them is that of Captain Tobias Lear, of Portsmouth, which, in addition to the skull and cross-bones, has an urn with flames at top and a rudimentary willow tree. This suggests that Homer sometimes used only the urn and tree as on the stone of John Hurd, Granary, 1784 — the young officer who 'ne'er gave his father Grief but when he died.' It is more probable that John Homer made this stone, because other members of the Hurd family are buried by side of John with skulls and cross-bones their only ornamentation.

There are eleven men by the name of Homer mentioned in the Boston Directory for 1796. John Homer & Son, stonecutters, had their place of business at Moore's Wharf, John living on Middle Street in a modest little house with sixteen windows, while his son William was not far away on Cross Street. There were other Williams and Johns, masons; Michael and Jacob, masons, and two merchants, Eleazar and Benjamin, the grandfather and father of Winslow Homer, the artist — all probably members of the same Homer family.

John

JOSEPH CRAIG, JR., OAKHAM, 1777

HEZEKIAH STONE, OXFORD, 1771

JOHN PRATT, BENNINGTON, VT., 1768

JOHN VINAL, SCITUATE, 1698

John Homer disappears from the Directory by 1803, and three years later his son William, the stonecutter, built the house still standing on the southeasterly corner of Myrtle and Anderson Streets, a four-square brick house 'much admired,' Mr. Chamberlain tells us, 'for its simple dignity.' William Homer died in 1822 and was buried in the Central Burying-Ground, but the grave of his father, Captain John Homer, is unmarked.

DANIEL HASTINGS

A very different standard for the carving of gravestones prevailed at the end of the eighteenth century from that at its beginning. In fact this century may be said to cover all styles of ornamentation. The stones of 1700 differ very slightly from those of 1670, and by 1800 allegorical pictures, portraits, urns, and willow trees were all being used. There were local workers everywhere, and the Boston stonecutters do not seem to stand as far above their fellow craftsmen as they did fifty or a hundred years before.

Daniel Hastings, of Newton, was one of the most popular sculptors of the later decades of the century. He was born in 1749 — when he was twenty-one William Codner was dead, Henry Christian Geyer and his son, John Just, were both working, and John Homer was making skulls and cross-bones for those who wished them. The later Lamsons, of Charlestown, and the Parks, of Groton, were exceedingly busy, but there was plenty of room for others of their craft. With the assurance of youth, Daniel Hastings stepped boldly into the arena, and like many a young man placed so high a value on his own skill that people accepted him at his own estimate and willingly paid what he asked. The first stone which the Probate Records mention was for Caleb Dana, Cambridge, 1770, for the engraving of which he received 15/8 d. Six or eight pounds for a pair of gravestones was not an unusual price for him to ask, while sometimes his bill amounted to twelve or thirteen pounds. The Parks at the same time for more beautifully cut stones were satisfied with much less.

Daniel Hastings, however, with his skill in portraiture, his neat carving, and conventional borders, appealed to a large number of conservative people, and he sent his stones all over Middlesex and
Worcester

Worcester Counties as well as occasionally to much more distant places.

The only person I have discovered who stipulated in his will that his gravestone was to be made by a particular man is the Reverend Benjamin Conklin, of Leicester, whose estate was settled in 1798. He writes, 'And it is my will that my executors provide decent, well-made gravestones, properly inscribed to be had at Newtown to be set at my Grave and my wife's Grave, which shall be accounted part of my funeral expenses.' Daniel Hastings, as far as I know, was the only stonecutter at Newton at this time and 'decent well-made gravestones' exactly describes his work. Among his stones is that of John Holyoke, brother of President Edward Holyoke, of Harvard College. He lived to be ninety-two, and so the artist depicts him, old and tired, his wings a bit irksome and not quite comfortable. But he has rested his chin on their feathers in the Centre Street Burying-Ground of Newton for a hundred and fifty years, and it seems as if he might continue to do so for at least another hundred and fifty.

The contribution of the eighteenth century to gravestone art was portraiture. This apparently was not attempted in the early days in New England, and it was well beyond the middle of the century that the death's-head or conventional cherub occasionally yielded the places they had held so long to a portrait of the deceased. William Codner seems to have been one of the first to introduce this new vogue, and, judging from the large number who wished to have their friends so represented, he must have had a clever trick of getting a likeness. He was followed in this art by Daniel Hastings, the Parks, of Groton, and some local workers in Massachusetts, and especially the last John Stevens, of Rhode Island.

These portrait stones are valuable, not only because they often give us the only suggestion we have of some minister, school teacher, or honored ancestor of our own, but because the artist supplied the lack of 'Godey's Lady's Book' and other fashion periodicals by carving upon them the styles then in vogue.

The ministers did not always have just the same cut of gown nor did they wear it with equal grace. What could be more carefully drawn than the one worn by the Reverend Nathaniel Rogers, Ipswich,

NATHANIEL PITCHER, SCITUATE, 1723

NATHANIEL PITCHER FOOTSTONE

PETER RIPLEY, HINGHAM, 1742

ELIZABETH RICHARDSON, MILLBURY, 1761

Ipswich, 1775? This is not gathered to the round yoke, as was more usual, but the front is carried straight to the neck and two finely plaited strips fall like a scarf from either side. With this gown we should expect the Reverend Nathaniel would don his most formal wig, and so he does — attired altogether as his people saw him every Sunday and as he would wish to be remembered. His face, too, is just what we should wish for a man whose preaching, as Dr. Stiles tells us, 'was Calvinistic, practical and very solemn,' and who 'in prayer was specially devout.' A less respectful critic was a college boy coming to Ipswich in 1773 with the Reverend James Manning. Even the Congregationalists were anxious to have the doors of their church open that this very distinguished Baptist minister and college president might preach an evening lecture, but the Reverend Nathaniel refused to have this done, and the young man wrote in his diary, 'Old Daddy Rogers their minister, is their absolute ruler.'

From other stones we get the dress of the everyday man — his best dress, to be sure — with the long, closely buttoned vest, and the velvet coat always worn open with the big silver buttons on the right side and even bigger bound buttonholes on the left. The deep round collar looks more comfortable than its starched prototype of to-day. We can supply the materials and the gay colors from the inventories, and it is easy to picture the man as he lived and moved upon the earth.

The military man, too, appears in his proper garb with his cocked hat and sword.

As we might expect, there is even more variety in the women's dress. Although all their gowns fit closely and all have the tiny waist which fashion demanded, they attain this desirable end in various ways. Many a bodice seems to be fitted with tiny tucks or plaits, while the skirt may be plaited also or perhaps closely gathered.

Anna Barnard, the widow of the Reverend John Barnard, of Marblehead, who died in 1774, was wont to wear a low, square-necked gown, closely fitting, hooked up in front, with straps over the shoulders — a very youthful-looking attire for a woman of seventy-eight. It is hard to tell whether she is wearing a close cap or only her own thin hair. But in the majority of the portrait stones of women
the

the hair is arranged in a pompadour. Jewels, too, appear, a chain with locket, ear-rings peeping out from a coquettish cap, gold beads, and sometimes ornaments in the hair.

Buttons form an interesting feature of these eighteenth-century styles, for it is only the men who wear them. The women's dress is invariably fastened with hooks and eyes. It is not uncommon to find a row of gravestones for several children in one family where the only difference to be discovered between the boys and the girls is the front of their little straight jackets, sex being indicated by a close row of buttons or by the lack of them.

CHAPTER VII
THE STONECUTTERS OF GROTON AND HARVARD

WHEN the Reverend Peter Whitney wrote his 'History of Worcester County' in 1790, the slate pits of Harvard and Lancaster were at the peak of their production. He says of that in Harvard: 'There are vast quantities of blue or slate stone. It leases to the stone cutters in this and a neighboring town for £6. 10/ per annum. . . . The stones are chiefly used for grave and tomb stones and are carried to a great distance.' This old quarry is on Pin Hill. It has survived its reputation and to most of the people of Harvard it is almost unknown. The stone is a very close-grained, durable, dark-blue slate which rarely cracks or stains, and is different from that of the Lancaster quarry which is softer. Mr. Whitney writes about the latter: 'In the north-easterly part of Lancaster is the fine and valuable and perhaps inexhaustible slate pit, furnishing slates and tiles for the roofs of houses, and most excellent stones for tombs and graves. . . . No slates equal to them have been discovered on this continent. Great numbers are used in Boston every season. They are also exported to Virginia, to Hartford in Connecticut.'

The Lancaster quarries, like those of Harvard, have long been un-worked. They are on the road to Shirley and occasionally are noticed by some interested passer-by, but the number even in Lancaster that know of their existence and former desirability is extremely small.

THE PARKS OF GROTON

William Park was born in Scotland and baptized at Balomach, a parish of Glasgow, October 7, 1705. Apparently he came alone to this country in 1756, a man over fifty, leaving his wife and sons in Scotland. His grandson, writing of him a hundred years later, de-scribes him as 'tall in stature, vigorous and athletic and discriminat-ing, well disciplined and educated.' He must also have possessed imagination to leave his home, where he and his sons were well estab-lished in business, to try his luck in an unknown land. It was scarcely five years since the Harvard and Lancaster quarries had been discovered,

covered, and in some way he found his way to them and decided that this was the place best suited for his work. Making his home first in Westford, he soon removed to Groton, where he spent the rest of his life, and where nine years after his arrival his wife and sons joined him.

Probably he brought many designs with him. He certainly had a greater variety in the quality and style of his stones than many of the other workers, and we find, as we should expect, a corresponding difference in their cost. His prices range from twelve shillings to eight pounds. His simplest stone was cut in a geometric pattern like that on the large double stone of John Holding, Groton, for which he charged, including transportation, £2.12/ in 1757. This is made on a poor grade of slate or schist, and for its size was very reasonable. A better illustration of this geometric design is the stone of Samuel Rockwood, Groton, 1753. This was among his very earliest work, doubtless patterned after those he had made in Scotland.

Joseph Underwood, of Westford, died in 1761, and the gravestone which William Park made for him and for which he received one pound sixteen shillings shows a different phase of his work. We detect in this and in the many similar to it an architectural quality which we might expect from a family of stonecutters who were builders as well. A very good example of this style is the stone of Susanna Hills, Billerica, 1758.

Another design which William Park was using at the same time is that on the gravestone of Benjamin Stone, Groton, 1761, for which his estate 'paid Mr. Park for Gravestones £1.6.8.' This stone shows many of his usual characteristics — the shape, with the point in the center, is rather a favorite of his and the delicate tracery of vines. But more than any other feature is the motto commencing at the upper right-hand corner and reading down, across the bottom, and up the other side, 'From death's arrest no age is free.' When unhampered by the relatives or minister of the deceased, William Park usually put this line somewhere on his stones — a line which was not a legacy to us from Scotland, but as far as is known an original contribution to graveyard literature from that early classic, 'The New England Primer':

I in

SAMUEL LOCKE, LANCASTER, 1775

EBENEZER COX, HARDWICK, 1768

CHARLES BRIGHAM, GRAFTON, 1781

Here Lyeth ye Body of
Mrs Joanna Herrick ye
Wife of Capt Henry Herrick
Who Od ye 5 1738 in ye 50
year of her Age

JOANNA HERRICK, BEVERLY, 1738

I in the Graveyard too may see
Graves shorter there than I
From death's arrest no age is free
Young children too may die.

At the same time William Park was using rather frequently a
curious type of death symbol which suggests a bulldog. Sarah Baldwin, Billerica, 1761, has this kind of image, and oddly enough it was
even selected as appropriate for a five-year-old child, 'fresh as the
morn the fragrant bud hangs withered ere its bloom,' as we read on
the stone of little Helen Cummings, Concord, 1759, and to mitigate
the savage bulldog face the cutter tucked a rosebud by either ear.

The beautiful stones of John Buckman and his wife in Lexington,
for which Park was paid £6.18/ in 1768, are very badly chipped
either by weather or carelessness. These perhaps represent his best
work, deeply cut, the flowers and leaves of the border standing out
from the face of the stone in quite high relief. The two stones are
almost identical except the wings, which for some reason the sculptor
thought were needed by John and not by Mary.

This deeply cut ornamentation is very characteristic of William
Park, and also the round face, small amount of hair, and pointed
chin. This same face is thrice repeated on the stone of Mercy Daby,
Groton, 1751, large for the mother, a little smaller for three-year-old
Phebe, and still smaller for baby Sarah. We see it so often that we
wonder if it bears any resemblance to Mr. Park's wife, Anna. It must
in any case have been his ideal, as it is his most constant representation of feminine beauty. Mercy Daby died five years before he
came to this country, so it seems probable that this flower border and
type of face was an inheritance from Scotland, as in fact all his designs may have been.

William Park also attempted portraiture. In Billerica we find
several stones which seem to have been his work, among them that of
the Reverend John Chandler whose estate paid him forty shillings in
1766. The Reverend John Chandler lived in Billerica, not far from
Groton, and the ministers of these country towns were well-known
personages in all the neighborhood. Whether the resemblance is
good or not, the sculptor seems to have caught the personality of the
man,

man, and it is easy to picture him as he walked up the aisle of the village church, broad-shouldered but stooping a little, gentle and slightly apologetic, with gown falling loosely about his attenuated form, and his wig and his bands both short.

The predecessor of the Reverend John Chandler was the Reverend Samuel Ruggles, who died in 1737. He must have waited long for his gravestone, for its handiwork is surely that of William Park, who was in Scotland for twenty years after the minister's death. It may be his friends ordered one after seeing John Chandler's, and either described the differences in the appearance and bearing of the two men or produced some drawing or perhaps an oil painting done by a strolling artist as a guide for his delineation.

When William Park, received the order to carve a stone for Judah Monis, it must have taxed his ingenuity to the utmost. A man of such an interesting history and important position required something both dignified and unique. Judah Monis had been a very unique person ever since the days when Cotton Mather had written of his conversion to Christianity, 'A Jew rarely comes over to us but he brings Treasure with him.'

He was a young man then. For forty years he had taught the Hebrew language to the Harvard students. In 1761 his wife died and, resigning his position in the college, he came to the small town of Northborough to spend the close of his life with her relatives. So it happened that his grave is in the little burying-ground there back of the Unitarian Church, marked by the stone made without doubt by William Park, which cost his estate three pounds, an architectural stone not shunning at all the terrible fact of death, but suggesting something beyond the drawn curtains and also the full fruition of the grain, 'sown in corruption, and raised in incorruption.'

The wife of William Park was Anna Law, whom he married at Glasgow on May 6, 1730, 'an industrious, intelligent and good woman,' as her grandson says. Perhaps when he left her in 1756 to make his home in the New World, he was looking forward to a very short separation. But it was nine years that he kept bachelor's hall in Groton, while she lived probably with her sons in Scotland. It must have been a glorious reunion in 1765, when she, with the two

younger

HERE LYETH Y BODY OF
IOHN COGESHALL SENIOR
MAIOR, HEE DECEAST
OCTO BR Y I . 1708 IN Y
90 . YEARE OF HIS AGE

JOHN COGGESHALL, SR., NEWPORT, 1708

Peter   fon of
Mr Timothy & Mary

PETER BANCROFT, AUBURN, 1786

HANNAH BRADLEY, NEWPORT, 1723

JOHN GOULDING, GRAFTON, 1791

younger sons, James and Thomas, joined him and made thereafter a better home for him. Two years later the oldest son, John, came with his wife and three little children. William Park lived for twenty-three years after his wife's coming, and he and his sons worked happily together until the partnership was dissolved in 1788 when the father died.

JOHN AND THOMAS PARK

John, the oldest son, was born March 15, 1731, and, in 1758, married Jean Stewart. Soon after he was employed by the Duke of Argyle to work on his castle in Inverary, and it must have been this very important and probably lucrative position which kept them all so many years in Scotland. Although John was a builder and took contracts for large stone buildings, he like his father found many moments when he liked to turn to some smooth piece of Harvard slate and make wonderful borders and beautifully cut letters.

He built the stone jail in Worcester, called the second finest stone building of its day, King's Chapel alone taking precedence, and when the Town minister died, the Reverend Thaddeus Maccarty, John Park was selected to make his gravestone. This, like nearly all Worcester's early gravestones, is hidden under three feet of soil on the Common, and we know only from the description of the copyist, in 1848, that it had the figure of an hourglass and wings and 'the figure of head and bust with surplice &c.' perhaps a better portrait of the Reverend Thaddeus than the dim oil painting that is now hanging in the parlor of his great-great-granddaughter.

'In testimony of his fidelity, the people of his charge erect this monument,' it reads, and the people of his charge were the whole town and to the Town John Park sent the following bill:

Worcester Nov. 12, 1790

The Town of Worcester to John Park Dr.
To making a pair of Gravestones for the Rev. Mr. Mac-
carty   £4.10.0
To do for Mrs. Maccarty   3. 0.0
To transporting the same from Groton to Worcester   12.0
                                          £8. 2.0

In

In Lexington there are standing two stones, the most beautiful which I have discovered for which John Park was paid. They mark the graves of Samuel Stone and his wife, and they cost in 1771 six pounds. They are apparently almost duplicates of those done by the father. Usually John's were smaller and less ornamental and his prices ranged from one pound two shillings to three pounds. Like his father, he undoubtedly had many apprentices, and the work which we assign to William and John Park may have been actually done by these younger hands. Sometimes they cut their initials on a stone — in one case, that of Thomas Prentice, of Lexington, the apprentice has boldly added, 'Engraved by Abel Webster 1763' to a very typical Park stone. Besides Abel Webster, the name of only one apprentice has been remembered by the Park family, that of Daniel Shays, who gave his name to Shays's Rebellion and may be responsible for some of the *S*'s cut on Park gravestones.

John Park built himself a house in 1791, the first brick house in that part of Groton which is now Ayer. This house still stands with John Park's signature, 'I.P. 1791,' hidden by an adjacent garage. He did not occupy it long, for in 1794 he met with an accident while building a jail in Amherst, New Hampshire, and thereby was arrested by death in his work.

His brother Thomas, born in Glasgow in 1745, gave his attention also to the business of making gravestones and carried on the father's work with much skill and variety. There is a great similarity of all that was done by the Park family, but Thomas perhaps did more of the elaborate work, the portraits and coats-of-arms. He lived until June 6, 1806, and like the other members of the family was buried in the village burying-ground in Groton. He was paid in 1778, by the estate of Colonel James Barrett, of Concord, five hundred and forty pounds — evidently in the depreciated currency of the times. The estate also paid 'for painting a coat-of-arms for a pattern for the stone cutter to work it by on the Gravestone £58.10/ and £15 for a journey to Groton to see about the Gravestones.'

The Colonel's headstone seems to be worth all this trouble and money. The arms cut upon it are described in Crozier's 'Armory' as the one which this branch of the Barrett family was entitled to use,

with

NATHANIEL INGRAHAM, NEWPORT, 1711

EDWARD ROSSAM, NEWPORT, 1724

NATHANIEL BOSWORTH, BRISTOL, 1690

NATHANIEL BOSWORTH FOOTSTONE

with its ermine shield and broad scarlet band forming a background for the three golden lions. Above are carved a death symbol with swords on either side, suggestive of the Colonel's calling. For James Barrett was literally called to unsheath his sword in defense of his country's liberty, being the commander of the militia at Concord on April 19, 1775. Near his grave is that of his brother, Deacon Thomas, who outlived him only about two months, and as we look at the kindly face engraved upon his stone we believe, what the epitaph says, that 'in him the Christian graces shone uncommonly bright.'

Without doubt Thomas Park also made the stone for Lieutenant Daniel Hoar, which was one of the objects of art which drew many to the Old Hill Burying-Ground when it was new, and of which Bentley says in his diary, 'it is very well executed.' This has carved upon it the same arms which nearly a hundred years before Hezekiah Usher had described as being upon the tumbler which he bequeathed in his will to his stepdaughter, Bridget Hoar, 'the Arms of a Spread Eagle with two heads,' and he adds, 'but I think one head for a body is enough.' Hezekiah wrote feelingly, for he had suffered much, judging from his will, from having two heads in his family in a day when there was supposed to be only one.

Like the Lamson family of Charlestown, the Parks continued for many decades in their chosen calling, and the Williams and Johns and Thomases of the following generations made urns and willow trees like the rest of the world.

JONATHAN WORCESTER

Before William Park came to this country, most of the grave-stones in Groton and vicinity had been made by Jonathan Worcester, a man a few years younger than Park, being born in Bradford on December 1, 1707. He died in 1754, thus leaving an opening in that part of Middlesex County for a skilled stonecutter. He seems to have been a man of one pattern — a pattern which he had inherited from the gravestone-makers of Essex County, and they in turn, through England, from the Romans of two thousand years ago. In York, England, there is a Roman sarcophagus which shows the same

geometric

geometric rounds which Jonathan Worcester and his forbears considered appropriate for the dead.

In 1756 the executor of Josiah Burge, of Westford, made a journey to Harvard for gravestones and paid 'the widow Worcester' £3.14.0. for them. Probably they were lettered by Moses Worcester, the son, who, like so many sons of those days, went on with his father's business. As we go into the graveyards of Groton, Harvard, Sudbury, Marlborough, and many other towns, we find these queer stone eyes looking impassively at us and we wonder what this curious face meant to those other passers-by of a century or two ago. Perhaps simply that the grave kept all secrets, in silence and safety. As we look at it, it seems to suggest a key — either to lock up forever the past or perhaps to open wide the future. Joseph Wheeler's stone is another example of Jonathan Worcester's work. It is one of the half-dozen stones remaining in the small deserted burying-ground between Westborough and Northborough.

Jonathan Worcester's inventory, taken in May, 1754, has among other items, 'To profitt arising from land in which is contained Rocks proper and convenient for cuting and shaping into Gravestones or ye Like being enforced by a Lease for a certain Term of time to ye said Jonathan Worcester dec'd, his heirs, executors, and admrs.' This lease was valued at £16.13.4, and without much doubt was for a part of the quarries on Pin Hill in Harvard.

JAMES WILDER

We imagine that James Wilder, Gentleman, of Lancaster, was never very robust. He seems to have been a favorite son of his father, Major James, if we can judge by his will, and doubtless he was allowed a free hand in choosing an occupation.

When he died of consumption, in 1794, he left among other possessions 'the remains of the first chaise ever owned in Lancaster,' perhaps once the property of his grandfather James, who came from Boston and brought with him the latest Boston notions. James, the grandson, in addition to the chaise also left chisels and hammers and 'one rubber to smoothe grave-stones with.'

His work was not noteworthy, and we are not surprised that, in

spite

spite of inheriting the larger part of his father's property, his estate was insolvent. He interests us, however, for he was son of a gentleman and grandson of a more important gentleman, who followed the trade of stonecutter, because it was what he liked best to do.

JOHN DWIGHT

A much more important member of this group of sculptors was John Dwight, of Shirley. He was born in Boston about 1740, and died October 2, 1816, when he was seventy-six years old. His father was a sea-captain. The 'History of Shirley' says of him, 'he was an honest industrious man in good pecuniary circumstances' — the latter a great asset for a man who in those days chose Art for his mistress.

John Dwight's work was very popular. It was always neatly done. His heads were sometimes a perfect oval with a tiny border of hair; at other times pear-shaped with hair like a twisted rope. The simply cut wings are at some distance from the ears, as if he intended always to fill in the space with palm branches, as he often did. His lettering was carefully done. The stone of Jonas Gale, of Holden, illustrates his work. He selected the darker stones of the Harvard quarry, and on the whole they have stood the New England climate extremely well and show less signs of wear than the lighter slates used by the Parks.

We find his work in Middlesex and Worcester Counties and sometimes quite far from his home. Brookline and Dorchester have some of his stones. Undoubtedly he was honest and industrious, as the historian says, but he may have lacked imagination or failed to give his fancy free rein. Having seen a few John Dwights, we can imagine all the others.

When the nineteenth century was young, many new stonecutters bought or inherited 'rights' in the Pin Hill quarries. But none of them carved the flowers or birds which the Parks had done or even the palm branches of John Dwight. The urn and willow were considered the correct mortuary ornamentation, and these were rarely carved at this time with either originality or skill.

CHAPTER VIII

THE THISTLE–CARVER OF TATNUCK AND OTHER LOCAL WORKERS

WILLIAM YOUNG

TATNUCK is a village on the northwestern boundary of Worcester, a beautiful bit of land with wooded hills and streams, and recognized from the earliest times as a desirable dwelling-place. When the Scotch-Irish, in 1718, came to Worcester in such numbers that they nearly doubled her population, many of them established their homes there. By the middle of the century, it was almost like Ulster itself, with the McFarlands, Blairs, Clarks, Youngs, and other families of the great immigration settled on adjoining farms and leading a social life of their own. The men, however, took an active part in the Town's affairs, and became prominent citizens.

Among their number was a family named Young, said to be of pure Irish stock, Presbyterians from the vicinity of Londonderry. The old grandfather, at the most conservative estimate of his age, was eighty-one when he reached Worcester, his son David was thirty-six, and William, his grandson, was a boy of seven. The local historians record the fact that this family were the first to add potatoes to the limited fare of the farmers, although these latter were slow in adopting them as an article of food, and surreptitiously threw them under the brush by the roadside when returning from the generous home of the Youngs.

Old John Young, the grandfather, sat by the fireside until carried to his last resting-place on the Common, while David bought land and built him a house, which, although enlarged when his son William acquired a family of his own, still stands at the foot of the hill where he built it, and the brook at its side rushes along as merrily as it did in his day.

David remained a yeoman, but his son William became a 'Gentleman' and a 'Squire.' His public life is written in the records of the

proprietors

JOSEPH REYNOLDS, BRISTOL, 1759

MARY GREEN, NEWPORT, 1715

ABIGAIL CLARK(E), NEWPORT, 1728

LANGLEY CHILDREN, NEWPORT, 1785

proprietors and of the Town. He was the Town Surveyor, a maker of the early plans and maps of Worcester, Justice of the Peace, too, Moderator for many years of the Town Meetings, serving on many committees, especially in the stirring days of the Revolution.

In all this we see the substantial, influential citizen, as practical and business-like as many another of his day; but if we read only these records, we do not know the real William Young. The other side of his character, poetic, imaginary, full of religious faith and hope, with longings to express himself which it was difficult to satisfy — this other side we see partly revealed on the gravestones which he made.

Undoubtedly this was not a kind of work which received much sympathy from his harder-headed neighbors. Their world was not peopled with invisible spirits, nor did the fairies dance on their green-swards. The flowers and birds did not speak to them as they did to him.

Still, once in their lives they needed his wares, and it was convenient to get them so near their homes. They could excuse this rather menial work on his part, on account of his valuable services in other directions. However, not one neighbor, friend, or descendant thought it worth his while to record the fact that he was a maker of gravestones; only the dry records of a few executors. That he wrote epitaphs was known in 1848 when those in the old burying-ground on the Worcester Common were printed.

He was a local worker with no point of contact with the carvers who did such beautiful work in Boston or in Groton. Undoubtedly he sometimes saw their work, but it did not occur to him to copy it. Unlike them, he had a book, Rudolph's 'Polligraphy,' which may have given him some hints about drawing, some proportions for the human figure, some suggestions about the correct form for letters or figures. This was only one book among many, for his inventory shows that he owned six books on law, six on history, seven school books, six on scientific subjects, surveying, navigation, etc., eighteen on religious subjects, and one book of poetry, Young's 'Night Thoughts,' a mine for epitaphs and forms and ideas for original verse of his own.

A majority

A majority of his stones were made for the people with whom he came from Ireland, the Scotch-Irish, and the faces which appear on them, crudely drawn as they are, suggest the Irish type. The borders or other decoration on the stones often have some adaptation of the thistle, the flower of Scotland, which, in the quaint floral language of the time, signified, 'I will never forget thee.' He drew his inspiration from the people, the flowers, and the birds of Tatnuck, with perhaps a faint remembrance of his own childhood in Ireland and the stories of fairies and Little Folk that he heard at his mother's knee. Perhaps he thought of the honey birds on the shoulders of King Curucha's daughter who lived in Tir Conal, when he wrought the stones of Agnes Crawford in Rutland and Robert Cutler in Brookfield.

It was not easy to identify William Young with the man who carved the many thistles in Worcester County. That they were the work of one hand was very evident, of a man who had very poor material, the kind of slaty schist of the Worcester Coal Mine, which, even while he worked upon it, would sometimes split so badly that he pulled off a layer over some small portion and continued the pattern over the broken part, as on the stone of Mrs. Ann Cunningham, Spencer, 1775, a stone which shows a style he sometimes employed, perhaps drawn from a copy-book which his son John had used when teaching the district school.

Worcester County was even less given to recording the purchase of gravestones than Suffolk and Middlesex, and there are only three cases where William Young is said to have been paid for them. The estate of Samuel Crawford, of Rutland District, in 1772 paid 'Wm. Young for a pair of gravestones £1.4.0.' The estate of Robert Goddard, of Sutton, in 1786 paid 'To William Young Esq. for gravestones £2.2.0,' and in 1795, that of James Tanner, of Worcester, 'pd Esq. Young for gravestones 0.48.0.' This last stone is preserved for future generations under the turf of the Worcester Common, but the two which we can still see are enough to settle the identity of the Thistle-Carver, neither of them representing his best work, but sufficiently characteristic in design and workmanship. There are many cases where he is paid an amount which might be for a gravestone, and in all but two of these the stones are without doubt from his hand.

MARGARET GEORGE, S. ATTLEBOROUGH, 1734/5

POLLIPUS HAMMOND, NEWPORT, 1773

JOSIAH PIDGE, SOUTH ATTLEBOROUGH, 1793

ESTHER HALLIOCK, MATTITUCK, L. I., 1773

hand. In these two, the payment was probably for something else, surveying, writing a deed or will, or other service.

The earliest stone that I have found which was done by him is that of Joseph Ayres, Brookfield, 1740, when he was a young man of twenty-nine. His latest was in 1791, an old man then of eighty years, but still his work was more acceptable to many of his friends than the urns and willow trees which the younger men were using. For fifty years he had taken from his busy life as farmer, Town Surveyor, and Town Committeeman many hours when he sat alone with hammer and chisel and carefully wrought in stone the images which crowded his brain. And perhaps as he worked his mind was reaching out for some new way of expressing the old thoughts of the certainty of death and the happiness in store for the saints.

Besides the quality of stone which he uses and the thistles which in some form or other he frequently introduces, his distinguishing characteristics are: the way he crosses his *A*'s, always with a point going down; his frequent employment of a dotted background for some part of his design; a head with a long nose which is often formed by continuing the eyebrows down, although this is not invariable; very rounded shoulders with extremely small necks; straight mouths, often only a line, and low foreheads.

On his earliest stones he used the head alone with a simple scroll border — the men being distinguished by a conventional representation of a wig, as on the stone of Joshua Nichols, Brookfield, 1759, while the women have a close-fitting cap like that worn by Mary Moore, of Oxford, 1761, the two stones being almost identical except for this treatment of the head.

It was not until about 1766 that we find him employing the thistle, cornel, tulip, and other flowers to beautify his designs.

The stone of David Thurston, Auburn, 1777, is a good example of his use of the thistle, the three-story adaptation being very much like the old Roman designs used a few thousand years earlier on their stone sarcophagi.

On many of his stones we find another very common, humble little plant, a plant which undoubtedly carpeted the woods and hillsides of Tatnuck in his time as it does to-day — the dwarf cornel or bunch-berry.

berry. So also were carpeted the woods and hillsides of the mother country, and very dear to these homesick wanderers must have been its starry faces and scarlet fruit. Many times he uses only a whorl of its leaves, four or five or six as his space permitted, but sometimes, as on the stone of John Graham, Spencer, 1776, we find the four-parted flower, and even less frequently the fruit, as he has represented it on either side of Sarah Moore's extremely tiny neck, Brookfield, 1761.

The brook which ran by William Young's house comes down from a wooded hillside and on its banks there must have been many of those quaint flowers called Jack-in-the-Pulpit. It would seem as if he had one of these before him when he made the little stone of Joseph Craig, Jr., Oakham, 1777, and carved the banner-like growth starting from the center of a leaf, the parallel lines perhaps indicating the stripes which, according to the ancient legend, this flower received at the Crucifixion, for it grew beneath the Cross. It, as well as the cornel, must have been loved by the early Scotch-Irish, reminding them as it did of the brooks and bogs of Ireland, where it grew even more abundantly. On this stone of Joseph Craig, Jr., William Young uses the Medusa style of hair, for Joseph was a child only three years old and had not attained to the dignity of a wig. His father, the Captain, was a man of much importance in the town, keeping as he did the village inn, and having at his death in 1781, among other possessions, two gray wigs, a scarlet strait-bodied coat, a silk velvet 'jacot,' and 'a silver watch to keep time.' The father, who lies beside his son, wears one of the gray wigs.

William Young was twice married. His first wife was Jean Foster, who died in 1743. He died July 7, 1795, aged eighty-four, which would make the date of his birth 1711.

Three of the four sons who survived him were physicians, John, William, and David. They all left Worcester, and no one of his family carried on his business as stonecutter. His grave is unmarked. The sentiment he often carved upon the stones he made for others was very true in his own case — 'The grave is God's Hiding Place.'

His name, however, is spoken to-day by hundreds of people who never heard of the Thistle-Carver of Tatnuck. His oldest son, John, settled in Peterborough, New Hampshire, and his son, another John,

in

SARAH HARRIS, PROVIDENCE, 1723

JOB HARRIS, PROVIDENCE, 1729

JOHN HUNT, RUMFORD, R. I., 1716

ROBERT WARNER, MIDDLETOWN, CONN., 1732

in 1797, went to Ohio, purchased land and founded a town which bears his name, Youngstown.

William Young's work was quite closely confined to Worcester County; with the exception of Pelham I know of no town outside its limits where his stones are to be found. He was a local worker who, unlike many of his craft, always lived in one place.

THE SOULES

Another group of men who did much work in Worcester and vicinity belonged to a Plympton family of good Mayflower stock, which possibly may account for the large amount of journeying done by them. I call them local workers, because there does not seem to have been a great demand for their wares except in the places where they were residing at the time. Just how many members of the Soule family made gravestones, it is hard to say. One who did was Ebenezer, son of Benjamin and Sarah Soule, born in Plympton, February 16, 1710/11. He married in 1733 Susannah Coomer and died in Hinsdale, New Hampshire, on September 17, 1792.

His son Beza, born in 1750, and perhaps Ebenezer, born in 1737, made gravestones. Coomer, too, another son, was probably of the same craft, and the work was carried on by younger members of the family until well into the nineteenth century. They used a variety of materials; while in Worcester, they seemed to be satisfied by that iron-rusty, soapstony schist which the coal mine had to offer; in Bennington they used white marble.

They had a variety of patterns, all, however, having much the same feeling and effect. The stone of Hezekiah Stone, Oxford, 1771, is very typical of their work. The embroidered hair, the line of the nose, forming eyebrows above the oval eyes, the heavy shadow under the chin, the straight, small mouth, and especially the borders with the funny three-story flowers and profile thistle at their tops, were all Soule characteristics. Equally so is the Medusa hair, as on the stone of poor little Elizabeth Caldwell, Barre, 1777, who 'died to the Greaf of a Fond Mother and the Blasted Expectation of an Indigent Father,' and also the scroll border and the star. Plympton and Plymouth are full of stones with Medusa hair, and Deerfield and vicinity where

Coomer

Coomer and Beza lived for a while, have many two- or three-story flowers and many similar heads with embroidered hair.

Coomer and his wife are both buried in Barre under typical Soule stones. She died before he did, and her stone, perhaps made by him, is much better than his, although both are of a regular Soule design.

The father, Ebenezer, moved to Hinsdale, New Hampshire, where he found a ready market for his work. Some of the gravestones in the early burying-ground there and in that of the near-by town of Brattleborough, Vermont, are of just the same pattern, even to the smallest detail that he used in Oxford, Holden, and Rutland, and other Worcester County towns. The slate of his New Hampshire stones is from a different quarry from those he carved in Massachusetts, and sometimes he replaces it with marble.

We find also that he supplied some of the people of Bennington with marble stones. We can easily discern his hand on that of John Pratt, Bennington, 1768, although the three-story buds have blossomed and the features of the face are more carefully elaborated.

A SCITUATE SCULPTOR

A very interesting stonecutter, because very different from any one else, is a man whose work seems to radiate from Scituate. There is very little in the oldest burying-ground there of his period which is not from his hand, and we recognize his distinctive ornamentation in Hingham, Cohasset, and other near-by towns.

The earliest stone in his characteristic style is that for John Vinal, Scituate, 1698, and all the Vinal family followed in John's footsteps and had their gravestones carved by this friend and neighbor. Some years later, there was a Jacob Vinal, of Scituate, making gravestones, and it seems quite probable that the carver of these interesting rosettes was also a Vinal. The most noteworthy feature of his work was his rosettes, made of sharp little triangles which seem to have been taken out with one blow on his chisel. These sometimes, as on John Vinal's stone, alternate with a very simple, heavy scroll. His lettering, too, is unique, carefully ruled and sharply and clearly cut. He was not economical of triangles when he made the stone for the
Reverend

PHILLIS LYNDON, NEWPORT, R. I., 1773

JOHN HOWELL, SOUTHAMPTON, L. I., 1696

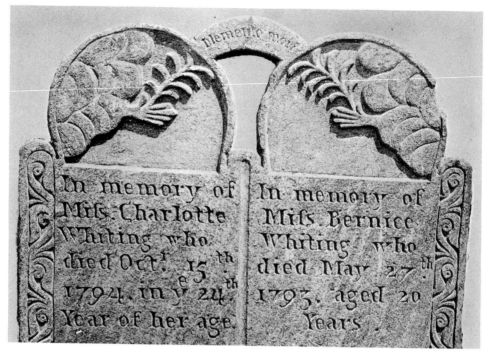

THE MISSES WHITING, NORWICHTOWN, CONN., 1794

JONATHAN ALLEN, NORTHAMPTON, 1776

Reverend Nathaniel Pitcher, the beloved pastor of the North Church, and they abound as well on the rather elaborate footstone. Unlike most of the early stone cutters, he knew how to space his lettering and his inscriptions are remarkably free from any interlineations or unpleasant crowding.

This man, or possibly a son of his, worked until into the fourth decade of the eighteenth century, although he gradually added other forms of ornamentation to his triangles, and sometimes he omitted them altogether except on the wings of the death's-head. His faces, too, lose their simplicity, and he adopts or originates that curious Plymouth County habit of replacing the mouth with a heart. Peter Ripley, Hingham, 1742, is a good example of this later work.

SAMUEL FISHER OF WRENTHAM

It is difficult to choose the most interesting men among the many local workers. Samuel Fisher, of Wrentham, almost deserves a place among the important artists of his day, for his gravestones were in great demand and very many of the burying-grounds, quite far from Wrentham, have at least a few of his stones — even the Granary has one. But having chosen the kind of border he would make, the kind of eyes, nose, and mouth he would bestow upon his heads, and the nice rolls of hair he would carve at the sides, he very rarely departed in any particular from his model. The stone of Ebenezer Cox, Hard-wick, 1768, is quite typical of his work, and has the added advantage of his signature.

Once at least he tried to be original and evolved the curious profile heads for Mr. Samuel Locke, Lancaster, 1775. But he could not quite manage the rolls of hair at this unusual angle and was better satisfied with the ears he put in their accustomed place.

It was Samuel Fisher and his son who made the Angle Monument which marks the boundary between the old Massachusetts and Plymouth Colonies.

JAMES NEW

A man of much more originality and skill, coming from the same locality, was James New, a late worker. He was one of a family of stonecutters,

stonecutters, his father John and his grandfather James having preceded him in the art of making gravestones. He was born in Wrentham, September 3, 1751, the son of John and Mercy (Adams) New. He married Anne Perry and died in Bellingham August 28, 1835. During his long life he lived in various places, Attleborough and Grafton being two of them, and his work is found abundantly in all the towns in the vicinity of his various homes. His usual gravestone was made on a fine blue slate, sometimes a clear gray, which cut down to a real cobalt, making an effective cameo. He carved on his simpler stones a sweet-faced cherub with level wings on a diaper background. This pattern is probably inherited from his grandfather, who must have made the stone for Elizabeth Richardson, Millbury, 1761. The rose and the level wings and the little pointed cap we find over and over again on the stones carved by James New, but there are many more elaborate and more interesting gravestones which he did. Occasionally he signed one, like that of Colonel John Goulding, Grafton, 1791. Here he thoughtfully labels the coat-of-arms for the enlightenment of the country spectator who might otherwise surmise that the five rampant lions had had something to do with the passing of the glory of the world for Colonel Goulding.

Nor was he afraid to try his hand at portraiture, and Charles Brigham, Esq., Grafton, 1781, in his scarlet coat as Royal Magistrate, and his white wig, shows a slight resemblance to his descendants of the third and fourth generation.

Equally interesting is his little portrait of three-year-old Peter Bancroft, Auburn, 1786, with his pompadour hair, his high collar and carefully tied bow, a real little gentleman of his day.

JOHN HOLLIMAN

I have found no stonecutter in Essex County who had more than a local reputation. All the fine early stones in Salem, Newbury, Ipswich, or Marblehead seem to have been made by Boston men. The county, however, had its full quota of gravestone-makers with distinct styles of their own. The rather crude, geometric design, like that which Jonathan Worcester carried up to Worcester County, was most frequently used, although others equally crude and geometric

often

often took its place. In Haverhill there is one of these conventional designs on the stone of Matthew Gannett, who died in 1695, and in North Andover there are others similar dated in the seventeenth century.

One of the most popular and original of the Essex County stone-cutters was John Holliman. He was living in Salem in 1722 when, according to the Town Records, he married Susanna Prentice. Several of his children are buried in the Charter Street Burying-Ground under stones which he must have made, and without doubt he was the John Holman [Holliman] to whom the estate of John Conant, of Marblehead, paid ten pounds for gravestones in 1746. These still stand and are like those of his children. His round heads with flat noses are amusing, and a peculiarity of his is fine chisel marks both around his design and on his backgrounds.

The gravestone of Joanna Herrick, Beverly, 1738, was perhaps his masterpiece of originality and shows extremely well his use of the chisel and his idea of the human face.

From Bentley's diary we learn that he was also an artist. Writing on June 7, 1816, he says: 'Visited the Woodbridge house, said to be one hundred and forty years old, to view Holliman's painting. He died about 1744. The great south-east room is panelled on the north side around the fireplace. The ground is variegated white and black shaded. The panels framed in white. Above in the chamber the ground white and red variegated shades, frame and panel as below. One beam till lately covered by a closet exhibits all the beauty of this man's coloring.'

In 1742, 'John Holliman of Salem mason and painter' bought a lot of land on Beacon Hill which he mortgaged back to the seller for the whole amount. Sometime later the mortgage was probably fore-closed, perhaps after John Holliman's death. Bentley's date of 1744 is too early for this event, as we know from John Conant's stone, but there is none of his work that can be recognized in Boston and the inference is that he lived and died a local Essex County stonecutter.

CHAPTER IX

THE GRAVESTONES OF RHODE ISLAND

RHODE ISLAND was the sanctuary of Massachusetts in the early days. There her unruly Quakers, her Seventh-Day Baptists, her Antinomians, and her unwelcome Jews found refuge, and there, too, her land merchants, as well as many of her substantial citizens, established homes better suited to their activities. There are many names common to the records of each State; many that we associate entirely with Rhode Island were once prominent in the history of Boston.

It is true of Rhode Island, as it is of Massachusetts, that the makers of the very earliest gravestones are unknown. In 'The Neck' at Bristol is a plain red sandstone with the inscription, '1696 Mr. R. Smith.' Richard Smith, who died in 1696, was Bristol's first Town Clerk and was also a mason and stonecutter. This inscription on his gravestone has been called his autograph, but is quite unlike the beautiful signature he affixed to his entries in the Town Book. Even if done by him, it furnishes no clue to his other work. He, like so many of the early settlers of Rhode Island, was a Boston man. In February, 1682, he signs a deposition in regard to 'a stack of chimnies' which he had built for Thomas Platt's house; the May following he was chosen Town Clerk of Bristol, a position to which he was annually reëlected until his death.

THE STEVENS FAMILY

There are many gravestones of the seventeenth century in Rhode Island, especially in Newport. Some of these, as we have already seen, were probably made by William Mumford or other Boston stonecutters. But by the beginning of the eighteenth century, Newport had a stonecutter of her own, the founder of a large and important family of that craft. His name was John Stevens, unfortunately a rather common name, and consequently it is difficult to trace his previous history. His first appearance on the Newport Land

Records

SIMON WOLCOTT, SOUTH WINDSOR, 1732

RUTH WELLS, EAST HARTFORD, 1744

CHARLES WOLCOTT, SOUTH WINDSOR, 1754

ELIZABETH WOLCOTT, SOUTH WINDSOR, 1765

Records is in 1705, when he buys a lot of land from Nathaniel Coddington, and at that time he is described as a mason of Newport.
There he lived and made gravestones on this same lot of land on
upper Thames Street until 1736, when he died on September 18, in
the ninetieth year of his age, according to his gravestone still standing in the Common Burying-Ground on Farewell Street. His wife
was Mercy, and his list of seven children begins with his son John,
born February 27, 1702, when he was fifty-five years old. It would be
interesting to know where he spent the first half-century of his life
and whether he was carving gravestones in that other locality.

This list of his children is copied in a manuscript volume of Bible
records owned by the Newport Historical Society. It begins, 'John
Steven's Book Dec. 22 1646.' Possibly this may be the date of his
birth, which would make him, as the gravestone says, in his ninetieth
year at the time of his death.

His own stone is unlike any other in the burying-ground. It is of
light sandstone, carefully cut, but in a style of work quite unlike that
of himself or his son. Some one wrote an epitaph for him:

> With patience having run his race
> Now Death hath set him free
> We wish he doth enjoy the place
> of true Felicity.

By his side lies his wife, Mercy, who died in 1745, aged sixty-six,
thirty-three years younger than her husband.

His son, too, had a book. Upon its first page appears his name
'John Stevens His Book 1727.' It contains accounts kept by this
second John and to this we owe much of our knowledge of the work
of both the father and son. It is a delightful old manuscript volume
of many dates and used for many purposes. He may have copied into
it items from an earlier book or perhaps from loose papers, for some
of the entries are made when this second John was only ten years old.
The stones charged for at that time must have been the father's work.
One such is that for little Nathaniel Ingraham, for which his father,
John Ingraham was to pay fourteen shillings in 1712, an especially
valuable entry, as it gives us the key to many stones fashioned by the

first

first John Stevens — his cheaper, everyday style of work. These are carved on a black slate, always with a head with hanging teeth and a simple border, sometimes like that of Nathaniel Ingraham and oftener of rosettes connected by a cord. This same unusual head is sometimes carved on stones having a fruit border; this, however, is in outline, all of the ornamentation, both head and border, being curiously suggestive of a school boy's drawing on his slate. As we should expect, we find these outline borders without the distinctive heads, not only in Rhode Island, but also in Boston, and even in Long Island. John Coggeshall, Sr., Newport, 1708, illustrates this combination of hanging teeth and outlined fruit.

In 1726, Jahleel Brenton was paid for a gravestone for Hannah Bradley. As he was not a stonecutter, and as a matter of fact had been paid as executor in another case for a stone made by John Stevens, it seems reasonable to conclude that Stevens also made the Bradley stone. Although the second John might have carved this, his father was a vigorous man of seventy-nine and perhaps was still an acceptable artist. The style of Hannah Bradley's stone is that of many made in the first quarter of the eighteenth century, like that of Edward Rossam, Newport, 1724. In this same style and similar workmanship is the little stone of Paul Simons, Granary, 1690, suggesting the possibility that John Stevens may have at one time lived in Boston.

Did we need further proof that the first John Stevens carved the stones like those of Hannah Bradley and Edward Rossam, we can find it in instances like that of Solomon Curtis, Tyler's Point, Barrington, 1711, who has a similar design on his headstone and the hanging teeth on the footstone.

In Bristol is a stone of Stevens workmanship which has the earliest date of any I have seen, that of Nathaniel Bosworth, 1690, fifteen years before he bought his lot of land in Newport. Both this headstone and the footstone which made up the 'set,' show very plainly the Stevens hand.

It is not so easy to see it on the odd little stone in Newport for Mary Green 'hew was born' in 1715 and died in 1716. That is black and rough. If done by the first John Stevens, it is a poor specimen
of

ABIGAIL HUNTINGTON, NORWICHTOWN, CONN., 1734

JOHN CHRISTOPHERS, EASTHAMPTON, L. I., 1723

MARY ROBINSON, NEW LONDON, CONN., 1753

OBADIAS PEASE, ENFIELD, CONN., 1766

of his art; it may be some other stonecutter carved the curious birds and the tempting dish of fruit. But the sculptor, whoever he was, must have been thinking of what would best please so young a child, and what could he have chosen more acceptable than the pile of red apples and the birds who are always just on the point of partaking of them?

Like many sons who followed their father's trade, the second John Stevens at first seems to use the same old designs, but as time goes on he modifies them to suit his own fancy. He discarded entirely the queer heads with hanging teeth and liked best a small cherub with wings rising high above the head on either side.

In 1727, he writes in his notebook:

John Clark, gunsmith,	
to a pr. G. S. for your child	1. 0.0.
To one gravestone for your wife and epitaph	3.17.6.
To one pr. for your child and epitaph	2. 6.4.

Abigail Clark's gravestone is still in the Common Burying-Ground at Newport and near it that of her son Samuel, both perhaps dying a year later than the first child, who had a cheaper stone; both those of Abigail and little Samuel are quite typical of the second John's work. Here we see the oval head deeply sunk in the wings and the rather expensive epitaph reads:

Adieu Vain World — Vain World adieu
I come ye Blest, I come to you.

It was the second John who carved very many of the horizontal slabs with coats-of-arms which are found in all the burying-grounds of Newport, and the account book records the bills for those of the period which it covers. One charge is to

George Wanton Nov. 21 1726	
To one Tomb Stone	£10. 0.0
to Cutting one Cwoat of arms	4. 0.0
to an Epoteph of 528 Letters 2d. per letter	4. 8.0
to stone for the foundation	0.10.0
to setting up the Tomb Stone	1. 8.0

In another bill to Mr. John Cupitt he itemizes, 'to cutting two cherubim's cherubim's heads, 0.12.0,' and the cherubim's heads are still to be seen on John Cupitt's tombstone in the little burying-ground on Golden Hill Street, in Newport.

In Bristol there is a very interesting, finely carved armorial stone for Joseph Reynolds, 1759, which has the Stevens border as well as his good workmanship. It is on a light sandstone, but, in spite of this perishable material, the fur of Mr. Reynolds's gray foxes is sharply delineated and their slanting eyes are still bright.

John Stevens gives us glimpses in his account book of his many other lines of activity. Among them one of his most common charges is for making and repairing shoes — again the seemingly incongruous trades of stonecutter and cordwainer are carried on by the same individual; he also built houses, plastered them, made stone chimneys and hearths, and, most surprising of all, charged 'for schooling for your children.'

Part of the old account book was utilized by his son, the third John, for lists of books he had read, and one or the other of them made careful drawings of borders of scrolls and flowers which might be useful to him and copies of epitaphs which pleased him. One of these latter as it is jotted down without correction reads:

> Hir Soll is Fled
> She Gorn to Dust
> but rise agane
> She Shurly must
> When Jesus with his
> Lovly vorce
> Corlls forth his Sants
> For to Rejoice.

John Stevens, Second, married Elizabeth Wood. He died on April 17, 1778, and, as far as I know, his grave is unmarked, nor is there any stone to the memory of his wife or other members of his family.

Another son of the first John Stevens also made gravestones, Captain William, born in 1710. He lived in Newport until about 1775, when, perhaps because of his Tory sympathies, he went elsewhere. He married Anne Bull whose brother was also a stonecutter and a Tory. In 1794 he died in Alexandria, Virginia. His work, as far

as

JEDIDIAH DEWEY, BENNINGTON, VT., 1778

MANNING CHILDREN, NORWICHTOWN, CONN., 1759

HEZEKIAH HUNTINGTON, NORWICHTOWN, CONN., 1773

JOHN HURLBUT, EAST HARTFORD, 1778

as I have found it, is much like that of his brother. He may have made the stone of Captain Pollipus Hammond, who died in 1773 — it is very similar to others for which he was paid. It is certainly of Stevens workmanship, but like many in Newport it is badly cracked and stained.

Captain Pollipus Hammond was one of the pillars of the church over which Dr. Stiles was pastor. For years he had been a 'Guinea Captain,' and probably many of the slaves owned in Newport before the Revolution were brought in by him. Dr. Stiles writes, 'I have reason to think that if he had his life to live over again he would not choose to spend it in buying and selling the human species.' He probably found much more pleasure in doing his joiner's and cabinet work and using his 'all sorts of Tools,' for he was 'a man who could turn his hand to anything.' 'God had blessed him with a good estate,' probably acquired in the slave trade, and to read Dr. Stiles's record in his diary it is apparent that in Captain Pollipus Hammond we discover an almost perfect man, 'punctual, upright and honest' with just one 'Flie in the Oyntment, the Disposition to exaggerate and tell marvellous Stories of Dangers, Travels, &c. in all other things was of a sober and good moral character. . . .' A very calm, peaceful man he was, whom everybody loved, and as we look at the calm, peaceful face on his gravestone we wish those stone lips would open and tell us some of 'the marvellous stories of what he had seen and heard in his Voyages and Travels.'

The third John Stevens, son of John and Elizabeth Wood, married on September 22, 1745, Elizabeth Smith. I have not found the dates of either his birth or death. For thirty years, more or less, he worked with his father, and unless we find his signature upon a stone it is difficult to decide which of the two made it. Perhaps it was the father who used the device of the scythe which in partnership with the hourglass seems to have cut short so many lives. This was a very favorite design at one period of the Stevens art, but does not seem to have been used much after the death of the second John.

On many of the stones of the third John there is either at the bottom or on the back the words, 'Cut by John Stevens Junr.' He liked to use a large piece of slate on which he drew, with a finely
pointed

pointed chisel, an aristocratic head, intended doubtless for a representation of the deceased, with borders of roses and scrolls and other conventional patterns. Mrs. Esther Halliock, Mattituck, Long Island, 1773, has one of his characteristic gravestones. Less than a month after her death, Phillis Lyndon died in Newport — Governor Lyndon's negro servant and probably bought by him from Captain Pollipus Hammond. She was a member of the church of which the Reverend Ezra Stiles was pastor and so was her husband, Zingo Stevens, negro servant to John Stevens himself. Dr. Stiles was much interested in this humble member of his flock and records in his diary Brother Zingo's earnest concern for his wife and children which he 'feels was blessed to her saving Conversion.' And he adds: 'She was brought hither out of Guinea 1759 aged 13 or 14 and has lived in Governor Lyndon's family ever since. She was always free from the common vices and especially since her profession has walked soberly and exemplarily.'

John Stevens made her a good gravestone. She wears her turban just as she did when she served the Governor, but her face bears the aristocratic touch which this sculptor always gives. The baby in her arms, broken though it is, shows the curly hair and flat nose which he hesitated to bestow on Phillis.

It is interesting to wander through this far-off corner of the Farewell Street Burying-Ground where the colored people were laid by themselves, to see the many attempts which John Stevens made to represent these sons and daughters of Ethiopia and Guinea. He never fails to give them the arched nostril and the straight nose of his ideal, but he does not forget to surround the heads of both the men and women with closely curling hair. Perhaps Zingo and his son Prince helped him in his work and liked to see the faces grow under his hand, not so much representing the children of their race as they had been, but as they expected they would be in their new surroundings.

John Stevens, Third, put an advertisement in the 'Newport Mercury' in 1781, in which he says, 'The stone in which he works is allowed by the best of judges to be superior to any commonly found in America.' I do not know where he found it, but as we see his

stones

JOSHUA DICKINSON, BELCHERTOWN, 1793

ESTHER WILLIAMS, DEERFIELD, 1800

SARAH OLMSTED, EAST HARTFORD, CONN., 1785

JOHN TRUMBULL'S CHILDREN, NORWICHTOWN, CONN., 1794

stones to-day we find many breaks and cracks which mar the beauty of his lightly cut and very delicate work.

After the death of the third John, his sons, grandsons, and great-grandsons made gravestones on the same lot of land which the first John had purchased of Nathaniel Coddington in 1705. The last of the Stevens stonecutters died in 1900 — two hundred years at least since the first of the name was using the little square-headed hammer which is still owned by his successors.

CAPTAIN JOHN BULL

Contemporaneous with John and William Stevens of the second generation was Captain John Bull. Like many people in Newport he was descended from a governor, Governor Henry Bull, being the son of Henry and Phebe (Coggeshall) Bull. He was born September 8, 1734, married August 18, 1769, Ruth Cornell, of Middletown, Rhode Island, and died November 28, 1808. He was brother-in-law of William Stevens, who had married his sister Anne.

In 1775 he removed his family and business to Middletown, as is stated in his advertisement, to 'the house formerly improved by James Phillipps where any person may be supplied with Tomb or Gravestones of the best black slate.' His work is not unlike that of the Stevens family, but there is a breeziness about his faces which they lack. In the Common Burying-Ground one of the stones which quickly catches the eye is a very long black slate, divided into six sections, one for each of the six little children of William and Sarah Langley, the oldest of the six being 'aged 21 months.' Each one of the sections is an exact replica of the others, having one of the faces which John Bull liked best to draw, faces which we find in many a burying-ground in Rhode Island and Long Island and which no one else made in just that way.

THE TINGLEYS

Providence has some notable stones in the old North Cemetery — most of them belonging to the first half of the eighteenth century. Some were made by the Stevenses of Newport, more by the near neighbors of Providence, the Tingleys of Attleborough, others probably

ably by her own local workers. One stonecutter, John Anthony
Angell, died in Providence in 1756. I have not identified his work,
but at his death he left gravestones which were apprised at eighty
pounds.

The Tingleys, father, son, and grandson, all named Samuel, lived
in South Attleborough. In 1811 two great-grandsons of the first
Samuel moved to Providence, where the business of making gravestones is still carried on under the name of Tingley. Although
Massachusetts men, they filled the old burying-grounds of Rhode
Island with the products of their skill. A peculiarity of much of their
work is the hairless head, which, although commonly used by them,
was often replaced by a rounder, curly-headed cherub. In the large
burying-ground of South Attleborough we discover many stones, including some for various members of the Tingley family, which were
very evidently done by one man or, more correctly, by one family.
That of Mrs. Margaret George, 1734/5, is a rather elaborate specimen of this style of work; while later, in 1793, we recognize the same
type in the gravestone of Josiah Pidge, signed 'S. Tingley Sculpr.' —
the third Samuel and the father of the promoters of the Providence
firm. Providence had always been a good customer of theirs and they
gave her of their best. Judging from the borders and the cherub's
heads on many of the armorial stones in the old North, they probably
were Tingley carvings.

Undoubtedly the Harris family were fond of their coat-of-arms, as
it appears quite frequently on their stones from 1723 to 1745. Some
of them, however, were not especially partial to the stiff ancestral
birds one over another in a vertical row, as we see them carved for
Sarah Harris in 1723 and so they employed a skillful stonecutter,
probably a Tingley, to bestow on them more natural grace. How well
he succeeded the stone of Job Harris bears witness, with its happier
birds partaking of the fruit of the vine, an emblem of Job's blessed
existence in a future life. We do not know these Harrises of the past,
but we like the ones who were looking forward to the joys of heaven
better than those who looked back to the pomp and circumstance of
this life.

The material used by the Tingleys shows no little variety. Much
of

of their early work is on a light, smooth slate, nor unlike that used nearer Boston. Later they sometimes worked on the greenish slate which so abounds in Plymouth and Bristol Counties — an unfortunate material — and on other schists and light-colored sandstones. They were among the first in southern New England to use marble, bringing the white limestone from Lime Rock, Rhode Island, to South Attleborough, a distance of about fifteen miles, where they had a sawmill for cutting it into the proper shapes. The burying-ground there was part of their farm and the trench which runs along its side was made by them for transporting this limestone.

Their work often resembles that of the Stevens family of Newport, so closely sometimes that it is hard to be sure to which family it should be assigned. Possibly the first Samuel Tingley may have learned his trade from John Stevens, a man forty years older than he, and well established in the business when Samuel Tingley was just commencing.

Some of their borders and even their style of cherubs seem to have been copied by others, perhaps pupils or apprentices, who lacked the ability and art of the Tingleys.

GEORGE ALLEN

In the village of Rumford there is an unusual gravestone. It is that of 'Lieut. John Hunt, Deacon of ye Church in Rehoboth,' who died in 1716. Half-hidden under the ground, and quite covered by moss when I found it, is the inscription, 'G. Allen Sculpt.' This is not only a very early example of the use of this word, as applied to a stonecutter, but the stone itself, with its artistic composition and carefully drawn cherubs, is evidence of a higher degree of skill than those of that craft usually possessed. Two George Allens, father and son, lived and worked in Rehoboth. The son also occasionally signed a stone, but I have never found another that possessed the charm of this one made by the father for Lieutenant Hunt.

CHAPTER X
THE GRAVESTONES OF CONNECTICUT

THE sandstones of the Connecticut Valley were used as early for gravestones as the slates of Massachusetts. It is said that the oldest stone of that material now standing is that of the Reverend Mr. Huet of Windsor, who died in 1644. This came, we are told, from the Hayden stone pit nearby. Probably the early Haydens made gravestones, but they did not attempt any elaborate ornamentation. They and their customers were satisfied with thick, plain, straight-sided slabs with good, deeply cut lettering.

Lady Alice Fenwick was one of those women of gentle birth who cast in their lot with the hardy souls who first came to the New England shores. Her life here was not long, only about six years. She died in Saybrook in 1645. Her husband, Colonel George Fenwick, returned to England, leaving her in an unmarked grave. At last, in 1679, more than thirty years after her death, the following receipt was entered in the town records of Saybrook:

April 2, 1679,
    Received of Thomas Buckingham of Saybrook, agent for Benjamin Batten, Esq. of London and in payment for the Tombe Stone of the Lady Alice Bolter late of Saybrook; That is to say the full and just summe of seven pound Sterling. I say Received by me
Matthew Griswold
Junior

As the Lady Alice Fenwick is called Lady Alice Bolter in this receipt, it would seem as if Benjamin Batten, Esq., was acting in this matter for the relatives of her first husband, Sir John Boteler; Colonel Fenwick had died many years previously. The Lady Alice's stone consequently dates from about 1679, but apparently had no inscription or date placed upon it until many years later. It is still to be seen in Saybrook, an example of a red sandstone of an early date.

There is a tradition that the first Matthew Griswold was also a stonecutter and made the gravestones for his father-in-law, the
Honorable

HOLMES CHILDREN, EAST GLASTONBURY, CONN., 1795

JAMES BRECKINRIDGE, BENNINGTON, VT., 1783

THOMAS ROBERTS, NEWBURYPORT, 1782

ELIZABETH NORTON, DURHAM, CONN., 1773

Honorable Henry Wolcott, still standing in the Windsor Burying-Ground. Both the stones, those of Lady Alice Fenwick and of Henry Wolcott, are heavy tombs with no ornamentation except the inscription.

Before many years the Connecticut stonecutters became more ambitious. Hampered as they were by their material, they could not even attempt the fine scrolls and the delicately carved faces and hair, or the flowers and birds which were possible on slate. But they could get bold effects, heavy scrolls, faces with much expression, though not usually beautiful, and curious geometrical figures. They even attempted coats-of-arms, and there is still standing on Long Island a badly worn, heavy red sandstone with the arms of Major John Howell, who died in 1696.

A FEW EARLY STONECUTTERS

It is not easy to name the early workers of Connecticut — sometimes we find that the quarryman is paid for a stone, perhaps lettered by some skilled workman of his own. Still we can recognize the work of some of the early men whom we cannot name.

One of the earliest has many stones exactly like that of Robert Warner, Middletown, 1732. He was working much earlier than this. The stone of Eunice Williams, Deerfield, 1704, is from his hand, as are many in Northampton. His work was very popular and is very distinctive.

There were two other men contemporaneous with him, each with an easily recognized style of his own. One of them chose a pattern like that of Simon Wolcott, with its full row of upper teeth, curious pendant wings, and unusual lettering.

The other man, who carved the stone of Ruth Wells, East Hartford, 1744, has a bolder border and face with no suggestion of teeth. He does not hollow out his eyes, like the two preceding stonecutters, but gets the effect of having the face look directly at us from the heavy outlines around them. He, too, did many stones which were carried far from his own home.

These men were closely followed by one who has been called 'The Hook and Eye Man,' and it would be hard to find a better descriptive
                                                                    name

name for him; his way of making his noses and eyes entitling him to this pseudonym. Mr. and Mrs. Charles Wolcott are buried side by side in South Windsor, and their stones are very typical of this man's work. They are of a gray schist as most of his are. The faces upon them must be symbolic of the jolly lieutenant and his thin and anxious wife. Did she wear herself out to the traditional skin and bones cooking good things for him? Probably not, for it seems doubtful that he acquired his rotundity by the food he consumed when we notice his tiny mouth.

'Hook and Eye' was extremely popular; all up and down the Connecticut Valley we find his gray schists and in many a town outside its limits. Sometimes he used red sandstone, but the schists were more to his taste. If a more elaborate stone was desired, he would rise equal to the opportunity and evolve quite extraordinary wings and sprays of leaves and flowers, as on that of Obadias Pease, Enfield, Connecticut, 1766.

JOSHUA HEMPSTEAD

Fortunately a rather early Connecticut stonecutter kept a diary, from which we can gather many details of his work.

Joshua Hempstead was such an important man in the community where he lived that it seems hardly courteous to call him a stonecutter. Yet such he was and, judging from the many entries in his diary, he loved the work, although at times he suffered from what would be called to-day 'an occupational disease' and 'is something lame with the humours falling down into my leggs but small sores. I stand up to work which I think occasions it.'

Miss Larned, the historian of Connecticut, says of him: 'He was at once farmer, surveyor, house and ship carpenter, attorney, stone cutter, sailor and trader. He generally held three or four town offices, was justice of the peace, judge of probate, executor of various wills, overseer to widows, guardian to orphans, member of all committees, everybody's helper and adviser and cousin to half the community.'

He was born September 1, 1678, the son of Joshua and Elizabeth (Larrabee) Hempstead. He married Abigail Bailey. He was always busy and usually recorded his doings for the day, but there are many entries which simply say 'at home all day.'

In

TIMOTHY LINDALL, SALEM, 1698/9

PAUL SIMONS, GRANARY, 1696

MARY HARVEY, DEERFIELD, 1785

ELIZABETH COGGESHALL, NEWPORT, 1773

In New London, where he lived, boats of all kinds were constantly coming and going. In fact, he had a whaleboat of his own. It was easy to get stones, already shaped into gravestones, from the quarries at Norwich or Middletown; easy, too, when he had carved them to send them to any desired destination.

November 30, 1725, he makes an entry which is typical of many. He writes, 'I went up to Lad's and agreed with Mr. Hartshorne for 10 pr. of gr. stones, 3 pr. large of about 20/ price and ye other 10/ 12/ and 15/ and I am to pay him in Wooll, to let him have 100£ and to take it out in Stones.' He most frequently pays in wool eight or ten pounds for a pair of gravestones, although occasionally a barrel or two of bluefish seems to be a more acceptable medium of exchange.

After getting a new supply of stones, he usually spends quite a little time with them. His work on them he describes in various ways; one of his first proceedings seems to be to black them — apparently not always done, for he mentions red and black stones; but evidently the bright clear color of the Connecticut red sandstone was not desired by all of his customers. Then he spent days 'blocking gravestones,' 'cutting Letters,' 'marking gravestones,' 'engraving gravestones,' a term he used more often after he became Judge of Probate, a bit more elegant than marking or cutting.

He more than doubled the price, selling one pair when finished for forty-five shillings, one for a negro boy for three pounds ten shillings, one for six pounds.

Sometimes he sells a lot, or what he would call 'a jagg of gravestones,' to William Wheeler, of Stonington; as, for instance, on July 5, 1722, 'Mr. Wheeler hath agreed to take two four year old Steers and two cows for 9d. per week and I have sold him 5 if not 6 pr. of gravestones to be delivered in Stonington, one half in money and ye other half in pasturing and bords.'

These stones were probably ordered by William Wheeler for some of the Stonington folk, for the next December Hempstead goes to Mr. Wheeler 'to get directions to cutt gravestones.' He sets out November 12, 1724, for Stonington carrying with him, in Joseph Coit's longboat, ten pairs of gravestones, eight to fill an order, two pairs not sold.

Ye

Ye wind was high, [he writes] about WSW and a great Sea on the flatts was forced to put most of the stones overboard and yn got a shore. Lay at night under a Haystack.

13. In ye morn we went up to Mumford's on Mr. Winthrop's farm. Stayed for the tide to rise — got ye stones in about 2 o'clock and got up with them about six.

Probably he rather enjoyed this excitement unless he happened to have on his new cherryderry breeches which 'Coz. Fox' had made for him.

He does not tell where he learned his art, although the earlier pages of the diary make no reference to this kind of work. It is 1720 before he alludes to cutting gravestones. He was then a man of forty-two, and from that time until 1758, when he was eighty years old, he writes over and over again, 'I was at home all day Engraving gr. stones.'

Of the fifty or more stones which he mentions in his diary as having been cut by him, about twenty are still standing in the old burying-ground in New London, and there are many others there and in other places which we recognize as his work. Old Norwichtown has many of his gray stones and Windham's earliest stones were done by him.

He has two very distinct styles — one a plain red sandstone simply lettered, like that of Mary Robinson, New London, 1753; the other a rather rough gray stone more or less spotted with quartz crystals and sometimes stained with rust, on which he always has a very conventional border quite poorly done. In fact a good deal of his work seems to be done for speed rather than for neatness and we can readily believe his statement that in one day and night he cut eighty-one letters.

A Rhode Island sloop, coming from Martinique in 1723, was cast away on the shore of Long Island, and among the bodies washed ashore was that of John Christophers, an only son destined never to reach his home in New London. He still lies in the village burying-ground of Easthampton, where the stone which Joshua Hempstead put 'on board Capt. Ring,' for him still marks his grave — a stone like hundreds of others which he made, a fair example of his usual grays.
There

THOMAS FAUNCE, PLYMOUTH, 1745/6

JOHN FOSTER, DORCHESTER, 1681

ANN KILCUP, GRANARY, 1694

SARAH SWAN, BRISTOL, R. I., 1767

There are one or two stones in the New London Burying-Ground exactly in his style which are much too early to have been carved by him, unless they were put up by some relative long after the date of death. This is entirely possible, or there may have been some earlier stonecutter from whom Hempstead borrowed his design. The oldest of these is the stone of Peter Bradley, 1687.

Joshua Hempstead died on December 22, 1758, just eighty years old. Like so many of the early makers of gravestones, his own grave is unmarked. If you seek his monument, go to the New London Burying-Ground and 'look around you.'

BENJAMIN COLLINS

Windham and Lebanon, four miles away, were the centers of much stonecutting. Benjamin Collins was in Lebanon as early as 1722, when his son Benjamin was born. His work was usually of the geometric type and his material a poor kind of dark-gray schist mixed with reddish particles. He found big slabs of it and apparently enjoyed laying out elaborate designs over a large surface. Once in a while he signed a stone, our only means of identifying his work. The gravestone of Mrs. Abigail Huntington, Norwichtown, 1734, is a fair example of his art.

He died in 1760 and left all his hammers and chisels to his son Zerubbabel, who became a more distinguished sculptor than his father.

THE MANNINGS

At the time of Collins's death, Josiah Manning was well established in the stonecutting business. He was the son of John and Abigail (Winship) Manning and was born in Hopkinton, Massachusetts, on June 14, 1725. His father was from Concord, where nearly all his relatives lived. He must have known exceedingly well the borders of scrolls and fruit to be found in the old burying-grounds around Boston, as well as the death's-heads and curly-headed cherubs. But he chose to work in sandstone, especially in mica schist, and he had his own ideas as to the kind of ornamentation he preferred. His genealogist says of him, 'he is reputed to have possessed peculiar skill

skill in carving the faces so often found on headstones in burying grounds of his day.' These Manning faces made by him and by his sons and pupils still gaze at us from many an old burying-ground in Connecticut as well as occasionally from those in other States. I found one as far away from home as Charleston, South Carolina.

Sometimes he signed a stone. At the bottom of that erected to the memory of the Reverend Jedidiah Dewey, Bennington, Vermont, 1776, we can read from the tops of the letters, 'Made by J   M   .' The rest is covered by the cement walk, a good example of the un-importance, only a few years ago, of the name of a gravestone-carver. Knowing the Manning faces, however, we can without any misgiving fill in the missing letters. This stone is of white marble as are half a dozen others in Bennington, all done probably by Josiah. At this period of his life he may have wandered up to Vermont and stayed a year or two while he did this work. There are a few marble stones with his peculiar faces in Norwichtown and Lebanon, perhaps brought back by him when he returned to his home town. Although we find so many stones in his very distinctive style that it seems as if he must have spent all his time on this one pattern, there is another one rather differently conceived which is not uncommon. We dis-cover one of this kind in Norwichtown boldly inscribed 'J. Man-ning,' that of the wife and children of Simeon Waterman, 1764, also like most of his on gray schist. In the same burying-ground there is another more interesting stone in a similar style of work, placed 'in memory of three children of Mr. Samuel Manning.' Samuel Man-ning was an older brother of Josiah, also a stonemason, and very probably made this stone himself. Perhaps he preferred the milder faces of these little bat-winged heads to those his brother oftenest made, and he may have added the barnyard fowls because he knew the children, two and four and six years old, would have liked to have them. If Samuel Manning made many stones, they must have been in the usual Manning designs and not distinguishable from those of his brother and nephews.

Josiah chanced, at one period of his life, on a rather beautiful fine red sandstone, quite unlike the common variety. It is a very light red, shading into soft grays, and evidently it had a very desirable sur-face

ANTHONY GWYN, NEWBURYPORT, 1776

JABEZ SMITH, GRANARY, 1780

GRINDALL RAWSON, MENDON, 1715

JOHN GROSVENOR, ROXBURY, 1691

face for engraving, as all the work done upon it is as clear and sharply cut as if upon slate. Hezekiah Huntington, Norwichtown, 1773, has one of these stones.

On the reverse of Josiah Manning's own gravestone in the Windham Burying-Ground he has cut the words, 'This monument I made in the year 1800; in my 76th. year.' He died on December 16, 1806. Beside him lies his wife, Mary (Cook) Manning, whom he married on October 13, 1746. For her he wrought a curiously elaborate stone, the headstone and footstone being connected by a marble slab. She undoubtedly deserved this unusual memorial, for it is recorded of her that in addition to her duties as wife and mother, she read the large family Bible through 'some seventy-two times.'

They had two sons who were gravestone-makers, Frederick, born in 1758, and Rockwell, in 1760. Frederick lived in Windham as we glean from an advertisement in the 'Windham Phenix' for February 18, 1792, which reads in part, 'Frederick Manning, Stone Cutter, Informs the public that he carries on the above business at his shop in Windham in all its branches. Makes Tomb-tables either of Marble or Bolton stone, Gravestones of ditto, side boards of marble, marble vats for painters, chimney pieces, &c. — all in the neatest manner . . . cheap for cash or country produce.' He died October 21, 1810. I have not been able to distinguish his work from that of his father and brother.

Rockwell Manning lived in Norwich and undoubtedly very many of the Manning stones in the Oak Street Burying-Ground were made by him. He calls himself in his advertisement 'Stone Cutter and Engraver.' In East Hartford is the stone of John Hurlburt, 1778, which he signed very conspicuously and from which we can see how well he caught his father's spirit, with the eyes which always seem to be looking at us from behind spectacles, the pompadour hair with curls at the side, and especially the unfeathered wings, like the water wings the children use on the seashore.

Quite near John Hurlburt's stone is that of Sarah Olmsted, who seems to have just adjusted her water wings and is ready for the first plunge into the dark river, a plunge, judging from the expression on her face, as much dreaded by her as such experiences usually
are

are by an untried swimmer. Rockwell Manning died a few months before his father in 1806 at Canterbury, Connecticut.

JOHN WALDEN

John Walden, of Windham, was without doubt a pupil of Josiah Manning, for he uses the Manning face with scarcely any variation. In fact, we should easily accept his work as done by one of the three Mannings had he not signed at least one of his stones, that for the two sons of John Trumbull, Norwichtown, 1794. He lived only about a year after the death of Josiah Manning, his estate being settled in 1807. He had a son John who may have gone on with his work. Probably he also carved the hands holding out the palm branches to the victors in the battle of life, a design used several times in the Norwichtown Burying-Ground and twice on the stone for the Misses Charlotte and Bernice Whiting who died in 1793 and 1794.

THE SIKES FAMILY

There was a family of stonecutters who in the style of their work and the choice of their material would seem to belong to Connecticut, but perhaps the largest amount of their product may be in Massachusetts. The distinguishing marks of their stones are a well-modeled face, oval and benign, surrounded by a raised line which sometimes has hair beyond it; borders of grapes or ivy leaves or various arrangements of stars or scallops. They are made on a great variety of materials, rarely on red sandstone, most frequently on schist or other gray or white substance, sometimes stained with iron rust to shades of deep red or orange, sometimes on quartzite with layers of black cut as a cameo, and toward the end of the eighteenth century on white marble.

Their work, as far as I have found it, covers the years from 1769 until into the nineteenth century. Plainfield and the towns north of it on the eastern border of Connecticut have many of these stones, while New Salem in Massachusetts and Belchertown and Wilbraham seem to be centers of this style of carving. From a white marble in Belchertown, the stone of Mr. Joshua Dickenson, who died in 1793, we get the name of one man who did this kind of work. It is signed

'C.

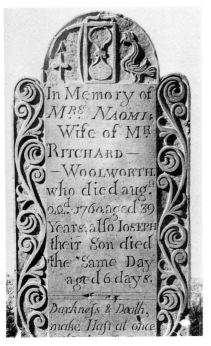

MRS. NAOMI WOOLWORTH, LONGMEADOW, 1760

GILES LATHAM, GROTON, CONN., 1788

WILLIAM HESCY, WAKEFIELD, 1689

REBECCA GERRISH, KING'S CHAPEL, 1743

'C. Sikes Sculptr.' Another in the same burying-ground equally characteristic is that of Hannah Dwight, 1792, and on her stone are the letters 'E. S.' Evidently there were at least two members of the Sikes family working at that time, perhaps sons of the man who carved the earlier stones in Plainfield, Connecticut, in 1769 and in Pelham, Massachusetts in 1770.

Some of the later Connecticut sculptors attempted portraits, usually cutting them in profile. One man, working toward the end of the eighteenth century, was very successful in getting good effects; his young children, with their bulging foreheads and delicately curved noses, look like children, his women wearing gold beads and other adornment are attractive, while his men are solid and portly.

In East Glastonbury there are many examples of his art. A very pleasing one is an immense slab of dark-brown sandstone placed to 'the Memory of Four Lovely and Promising Sons of Mr. Appleton and Mrs. Lydia Holmes.' Across its top we see them all, Appleton and Ozias, and the twins, Burrage and Calvin, and in their midst the tree with its lopped-off branches.

CONNECTICUT INFLUENCE IN MASSACHUSETTS AND VERMONT

There is many a gravestone as we follow up the Connecticut Valley made by men whose work we have learned to recognize in the more southern towns. The gray Bolton stones of Windham and Lebanon have yielded their supremacy to the red sandstone, which in turn was replaced by white marble. The towns on the edge of the Valley, like Brookfield and Deerfield, apparently liked all materials, slate, red sandstone, schist, and marble, giving a remarkable variety of color and style of work to their interesting burying-grounds, where Eastern Massachusetts meets Western. Western Massachusetts furnished the kind of stone that the Connecticut stonecutters were in the habit of using. Many of them wandered into this new field, where they not only continued in their old calling, but taught their craft to others.

The old town of Northampton on the Connecticut has a burying-ground which, with the exception of many late marbles, presents an
almost

almost solid front of sandstone, red, or often the lighter fawn color stained with black. Here we find the seventeenth century represented by plain, heavy blocks with no ornamentation save the inscription. Here, too, we find the work of many of the early stonecutters, but during the last half of the eighteenth century the local men supplanted them.

Among them one man, Nathaniel Phelps, seems to be the most notable. He was popular and original. Among many interesting designs carved by him is one on the stone erected to the memory of Major Jonathan Allen, accidentally shot by Seth Lyman, Jr., who in a winter's hunt mistook him for a deer. We could have wished for a more thoughtful epitaph than —

> who was slain as he
> was hunting on the
> 7th. day of Jan'y 1780.

Feeling in Northampton was exceedingly bitter over this occurrence and Seth Lyman, Jr., was tried and acquitted on the charge of deliberate murder. His son, serving under Major Allen, had deserted during the war and the father was known to have harbored harsh feelings. It is possible that the sculptor's own heart had been so touched by this tragic death that he could see the heavenly crown for Jonathan Allen being let down in a basket by celestial arms, while seraphs, blowing their trumpets, welcomed him to a happier hunting ground.

Western Massachusetts discovered marble quarries within her own limits and men from Northampton and vicinity moved to Lanesboro, where was one of the very earliest to be worked.

It was natural that these heirs of Connecticut workmanship and design, as well as those who were still living in that State, should be tempted even further by the more wonderful marble quarries of Vermont.

As we have already seen, there is some of Josiah Manning's work in Bennington. He was a chance visitor who tarried awhile with them, but preferred to live and die where he had for so many years made his home. But there were others, younger men, to whom the beautiful white marble of Vermont proved an alluring mistress, and
who,

MRS. TRIPP'S ARM, NEWPORT, 1786

SARAH HUBBELL, BENNINGTON, VT., 1797

PAMELIA MUNRO, LEXINGTON, 1770

BENJAMIN HILLS, GRANARY, 1683

who, once established on her soil, never looked back to the red sand-stones and gray schists of their earlier years.

Such a one was Zerubbabel Collins, son of that earlier stonecutter, Benjamin Collins, of Lebanon. Zerubbabel inherited his father's farm in Lebanon and his 'working tools.' His designs, however, were his own, and he found the inspiration for them before he left the polished little village of Lebanon with its governors and artists. He seems to have been a carpenter and cabinet-maker as well as a stone-cutter and he may have adapted some of his furniture designs to his stonecarving. Or possibly some embroidered bed set or curtains, or even a gay Chinese or Indian print or tapestry, may have pleased his fancy. Sea-captains were bringing home many treasures from distant lands — the 'trees of life' bore curious flowers not unlike those he carved. Although he never made two stones exactly alike, he appar-ently was well satisfied with his general scheme and never found any other that pleased him better.

There are a few of his elaborate flower and fruit designs in Lebanon and Norwichtown, carved on the gray schist used by most of the local stonecutters, but Bennington and Shaftsbury in Vermont are full of his work. In 1786 he was paid £7.10.0. for the stones for James Breckinridge, of Bennington, a very fair specimen of his usual style. He died in Shaftsbury in 1798.

The men who outlived him preferred simpler designs — Grecian patterns, grapes, perhaps only a few straight lines besides a portrait with closed eyes. The animation and energy of the old stonecutters gave place to the peace and rest of the new. The living man was no longer portrayed, but the sculptor strove to represent his spirit in its new environment.

Solomon Ashley, son of the Deerfield minister, was one of the earli-est to embody these ideas in marble. He seems to have lived a rather solitary life without the closest family ties, spending the greater part of it in his little shop. Here he sometimes moulded clay on his potter's wheel, sometimes shaped and engraved marble slabs. People came from a distance to 'go down to the potter's house' to order a pair of gravestones from 'Mr. Ashley' and incidentally, like the prophet Jeremiah, to hear the words of the Lord.

His

His stone for Mrs. Esther Williams, Deerfield, 1800, shows the simplicity of his design, while the epitaph touches this new philosophy of life and death; —

> Life is the Triumph of our mouldering Clay
> Death of the Spirit, infinite! divine!

CHAPTER XI
SYMBOLISM

THE gravestones of the seventeenth and eighteenth centuries carried a message to the passer-by both by the epitaphs and even more by the designs. We of the twentieth century can understand this message if we can close our eyes to the present and see them with the eyes of the past. Then we shall no longer think of them as grotesque or even quaint; with an understanding heart, we will get glimpses of beauty and sincerity; we will interpret them aright and find a lesson for ourselves in even the least of them.

Undoubtedly the people of that day passed many hours in the old burying-grounds which were usually close to the church — the most natural place for the noon hour to be spent when the weather permitted. The men, at least, were most punctilious in attending the funerals, and we can see many a man sitting 'upon a Tomb in the burying-place,' as Sewall tells us Mr. Morton did when Tutor Graves was buried in Cambridge, and saying, 'for aught he knew he should be next.' They meditated as they sat there on many other things besides the possible dates of their own deaths. And it was the minister and the stonecutter working together who suggested the subjects for their thought.

The ministers of the day and the educated people in general moved in a world peopled with Bible characters, the less prominent as well as the better known, and walking with these Bible heroes, apparently in most friendly fashion, were marvelous creatures of the pagan world. These they used to enforce their teachings and to explain the common, and especially the unusual, happenings of life, so that even the more ignorant members of society were familiar with the meanings attached to them.

The educated men recognized the inability of many among them, especially the women and children, to read the epitaph, however carefully cut, but all could understand the meaning of the death's-head, the coffin, pickaxe, and spade and the more comforting cherubim

ubim and scenes of resurrection. They were quite used at that time to discover meanings — hidden meanings we should call them to-day, but quite patent to them. What they saw at a glance, we can understand only by delving below the surface or hunting through some forgotten book. We should look in vain in our libraries for William West's volume on 'Symboleography,' but doubtless John Winthrop, Jr., who owned it in the seventeenth century, found it an exceedingly handy work of reference.

The ornamentation on gravestones was not only a means taken by the carver to express his sense of beauty and fitness, but even more to interpret the epitaph, or, if there were none, to teach the desired lesson in a way at once more expressive and more instantaneous.

The thoughts suggested by the carving of the gravestone can be divided roughly into five classes:

    I. A recognition of the flight of time.
    II. The certainty of death and warnings to the living.
    III. The occupation of the deceased or his station in life.
    IV. The Christian life.
    V. The resurrection of the body and the activities of the redeemed soul.

I. A RECOGNITION OF THE FLIGHT OF TIME

The symbol most frequently used to express this idea is the hourglass. Even the children, who had watched eagerly as the sand slowly ran down in the big glass on the minister's pulpit, knew that there finally came a time when it was all heaped up in the lower half and the sermon was over. And they knew about the sands of time and the little three-minute glass which typified the very short lives of which in those days there were so many.

The earliest stones, nearly all of them, have an hourglass. It is less common, but still not unusual to find the symbolism strengthened by the addition of wings, carrying out the idea of flight. A good example of this is on the stone of Paul Simons, Granary, 1690.

Father Time himself occasionally appears on a stone — always represented as an old man with a long beard with scythe and hourglass, as on the stone of Timothy Lindall, Salem, 1698/9.

On

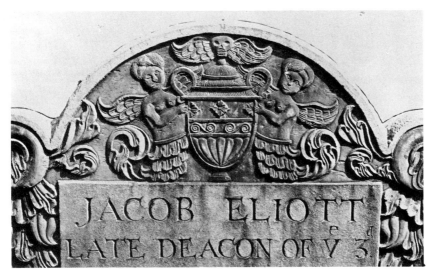

JACOB ELIOT(T), GRANARY, 1693

THOMAS NICHOLS, WAKEFIELD, 1765

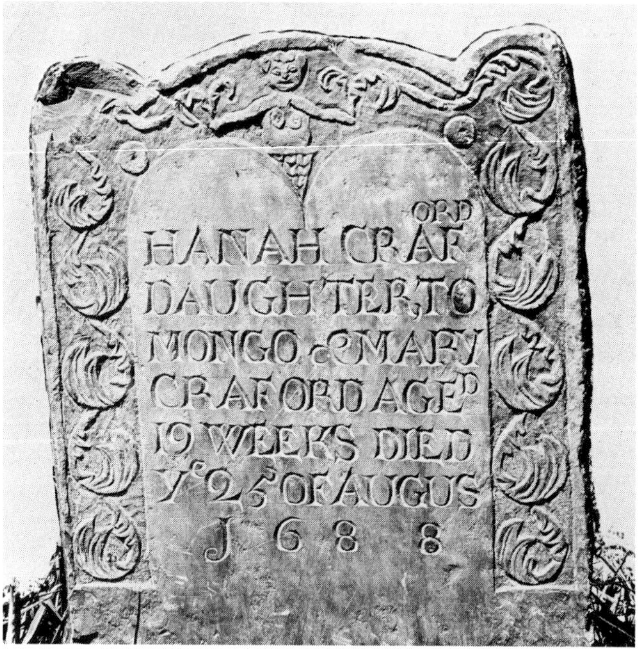

HANNAH CRAFORD, GRANARY, 1688

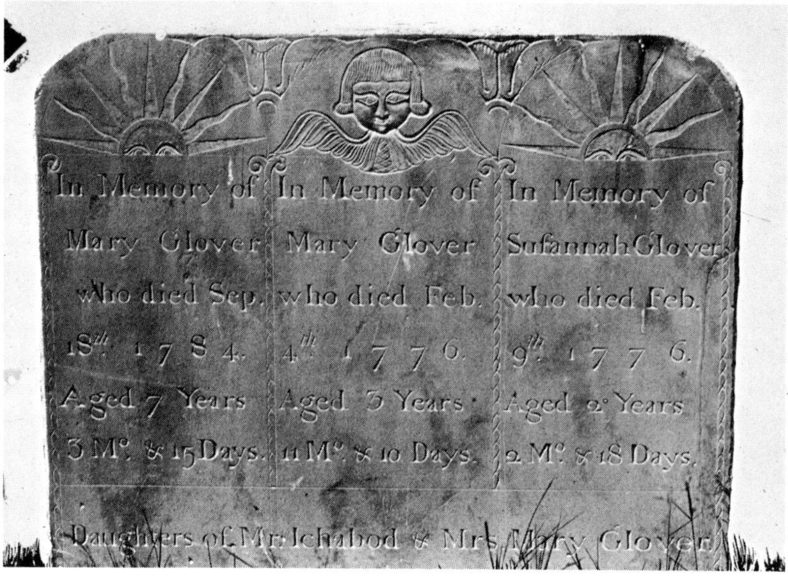

GLOVER CHILDREN, SALEM, 1784

On two stones, both probably done by that very early stonecutter of Boston, he is represented in action; his scythe is laid aside, but standing near him; in his left hand he holds the hourglass, and his right grasps the arm of death in a vain endeavor to prevent him from extinguishing the lamp of life of him who lies below. In each of these cases the candlestick rests upon the world, perhaps to show that the man is through with it and has risen above it. These are the stones of Joseph Tapping, King's Chapel, 1678, who, although only twenty-three, is described by Sewall as 'one of the most noted shop-keepers in Boston,' and that of John Foster, of Dorchester, 1681.

A few years before these two stones were carved, we find an 'Epatha,' the name at that time for elegiac verses, on the death of the Reverend Zachariah Symmes — where this minister is called the candle and his church the candlestick. Referring to God the author writes:

> that now he takes the candle, leaves behind
> the candlestick that it may be refined

There are several stones in Providence, unfortunately cut on poor slate, which have depicted upon them a light table — what our predecessors would call a stand — and upon the table a candle and snuffers. It looked natural enough to every one who saw it when it was first made. They all had light stands by their bedsides, all took a candle when they retired to their rest, set it on the stand beside the snuffers, and when all was ready snuffed out the candle and closed their eyes in sleep. The night had come when no man could work.

Sometimes the scythe alone symbolizes the passing of time. This was used especially in Rhode Island, where John Stevens often employs it. The stone of Elizabeth Coggeshall, Newport, 1773, illustrates this. Here the sculptor has cut the hourglass in two, the sands of time are gone, but Elizabeth still wears her coronet braid and her little vest with its simple decoration.

A Connecticut sculptor has embodied in some of his stones the early New England custom of the marriage trees. Even now we cannot ride very far into the country without seeing an old farmhouse with a big tree on either side of the front door, planted by the bride and groom when the house was new, and in a sense typical of their lives,

lives, a custom inherited from their Old-World ancestors. Such trees were planted by John and Elizabeth Norton, of Durham. Elizabeth died in 1751, and he, left alone, had carved upon her stone the two trees, hers already cut down, and his threatened by an axe held by a hand extended from the clouds.

II. THE CERTAINTY OF DEATH

The most universal symbol of this thought was the death's-head. Remember death was preached from all sides, in English and Latin, and the death's-head was another way of saying the same thing. In studying these early stones we see a great variety in the artist's conception of death; to some of them he seemed a rather cheerful personage, to others an anxious, sad, and often terrible being. Usually the death's-head is pictured with wings. Even less attractive and never extremely popular is the skull with its attendant crossbones. An early skull without wings is rarely found, the seventeenth and early eighteenth centuries preferring the conventionalized form.

The whole skeleton, although not common, was used over a long period of time. It brought death more vividly to the notice of the passerby than any part alone could do. It was occasionally combined with Father Time, as on Timothy Lindall's stone.

Sometimes the skeleton has darts in his hand — the terrible darts of Death, as on the rather late stone of Thomas Roberts, Newburyport, 1782, where Death has aimed at what he considers a vulnerable spot in Thomas's rather extraordinary anatomy, and the broken bud just beyond indicates to us that his judgment was correct and his aim sure.

Arrows or darts, even javelins, were sufficient in themselves to indicate death, a symbol especially vivid to a generation whose enemy compassed them about with their quivers full of them which, in spite of the white man's gift of lead, they still used with unerring skill.

Under this head, of the certainty of death, comes also the depicting of various articles which have to do with the disposition of the body. Coffins have always been used from the earliest time, usually closed, but sometimes open, disclosing the occupant, as on the stone of Mary Harvey and her baby, Deerfield, 1785.

The

WILLIAM GREENOUGH, COPP'S HILL, 1693

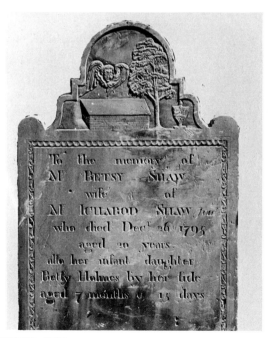

BETSY SHAW, PLYMOUTH, 1795

SUSANNA JAYNE, MARBLEHEAD, 1776

The pall, pickaxe, and spade were also employed constantly, especially in the earliest days. All these were designed to warn the living, not only to remind them that they, too, were soon to be 'as I am now,' but even more, that they should make themselves ready for their own speedy transformation.

'The New England Primer,' in a lesser degree than the Bible, had sunk so deep into the hearts of the people that it is not a matter of great surprise that we find its familiar lessons illustrated on gravestones. In Bristol, Rhode Island, the sculptor depicts the first couplet:

> In Adam's fall
> We sinned all.

Adam and Eve, the serpent, and the apple tree, are all there and, in addition, the Sun of Righteousness is shining in the Heaven, as it does in the Primer illustration for the third couplet:

> Christ crucified
> For sinners dy'd.

The familiar hourglass also illustrates a Primer verse:

> As runs the glass
> Our life doth pass.

And lest we should fail to recall the lines, the sculptor sometimes carved them upon the stone.

Occasionally we chance upon a crowing cock:

> Peter deny'd
> His Lord and cry'd.

Or, explained more lucidly by the Reverend Cotton Mather, 'The crowing of a cock was a monitor whereby Peter was awakened into repentance.' In the churchyard in Longmeadow, so near the street that all who pass by can see, is a crowing cock probably fashioned by Aaron Bliss in 1760, and still calling all to repentance as its maker planned it should. On this stone, besides the cock, there is a curious little figure on the side — possibly a spear, or perhaps a candle with the snuffer just ready to extinguish it — a scythe and the hourglass, the latter having all the sand piled up in the lower half.

Aaron

Aaron Bliss, who worked lovingly and conscientiously on the red sandstones of Longmeadow, did not hesitate to be more severe in urging the youth of the town to repent than his crowing cocks, and we find on the court records a complaint which he lodged against Oliver Bliss, a minor, who 'did on the 13th day of February at his dwelling utter one profane oath . . . which is contrary to Law and the Peace of the Commonwealth and the Laws of the same.' This profane young Oliver was fined sixty-six cents.

III. STATION IN LIFE OR THE OCCUPATION OF THE DECEASED

First in importance among these is the coat-of-arms, a dear possession of the early settlers when they were entitled to it, and so greatly desired by those who were not that the business of satisfying this desire was successfully carried on in Boston for many years. A fine example of a seventeenth-century stone bearing a coat-of-arms is that of John Grosvenor, Roxbury, 1691. From this early period until the close of the nineteenth century there are many such sculptures in our burying-grounds. The majority of them are on the flat tombstones or on the tablestones of the well-to-do.

Military trappings are used for the same purpose. On the stone of Sarah Cole, Warren, Rhode Island, 1770, there is a trim, self-satisfied young gentleman in dress uniform and wig, who without doubt was Sarah's husband, Lieutenant Isaac, who survived her. It would be quite in keeping with the self-effacement of the loving wives of that day had she chosen to have her memorial thus adorned. But when we chance upon the stone of Deacon Josiah Cushing, Rehoboth, 1787, and see represented thereupon the face of a cheerful lady smugly wearing her gold beads and locket, we decide that honors were even, at least on gravestones, in the eighteenth century.

Captain Anthony Gwyn, attired in his uniform and three-cornered hat, with his sword in his hand, stands eternally young in Saint Paul's Church-yard, Newburyport, although the stone tells us he had passed threescore years when he died on December 29, 1776.

As the military uniform denoted the soldier, so the ship indicated the navy and honorable service therein. The Continental ship Trumbull, built in Connecticut, sailed on her first cruise in April, 1780.

MARTHA GREEN, HARVARD, 1770

JONAS CLARK, CHELMSFORD, 1770

SARAH PORTER, HADLEY

CHARLES BARDIN, NEWPORT, 1773

1780. Battered, with fallen masts and tattered rigging, she crept into Boston Harbor the following June. After capturing several prizes off Bermuda, she fell in with a British ship and there followed a battle, desperate on both sides, about which one of her survivors writes, 'Upon the whole there has not been a more close, obstinate and bloody engagement since the war. I hope it wont be treason if I dont except even Paul Jones, all things considered we may dispute titles with him.' Thirty-nine of her crew of two hundred were killed or wounded, and among the desperately wounded she brought back to Boston was Jabez Smith, a young lieutenant. He died a few days later on June 28, 1780, and was buried in the Granary, where, 'anchored in the Haven of Rest' with the stars and stripes flying from her stern, the ship Trumbull still marks his grave. A few years after his death she was captured by British ships, condemned, and cut up for firewood. Her service in the Revolution covered a period of only a year and a half, but her short existence was a strenuous one and she earned the honor of having this memorial to her memory as well as to that of her lieutenant.

Sometimes the ship was used over the grave of a sea-captain or mariner, as on the red sandstone put up in memory of Captain Giles Latham, Groton, Connecticut, 1788.

It was not only the soldier whose calling was indicated by his dress. The minister often can be recognized by his gown and bands, or only by the bands, as in the portrait of the Reverend Grindall Rawson, who died in Mendon in 1715. I do not know that there is any other portrait of Grindall Rawson, but this vigorous carving by William Codner suggests a more live personage than the oil paintings of his father, Edward Rawson, or of his sister Rebecca. He may not have been richly endowed with the Christian virtue of humility, but he had many occasions for pride. He could be proud of his family and its high position in the Old World, proud of bearing the name of Archbishop Edmund Grindall, of Canterbury Cathedral, proud of his father's distinguished services as Secretary of the Province, and even more proud of his own high attainments in the field of learning, far above those of the majority of his associates. He must have made a fine appearance when he preached to the Indians in their own language,

guage, 'Of which,' says Mather, 'he was a master that has scarce an equal,' and also in 1709, when he delivered the Election Sermon in Boston and chose so unusual a text that we wonder whether he really found it in the Bible, 'Before your feet stumble upon the dark Mountains.'

There seems to have been nothing petty about him — the real man bore the accidents which befell him as calmly as the stone man does the trifling loss of his nose; and, as we look at him, we do not mind this loss — we see behind the work of the sculptor the soul of Grindall Rawson, imperious and confident.

A very humble symbol, conceived in quite a different spirit from the coat-of-arms, military trappings, or even the minister's gown, is the scallop shell emblematic of our earthly pilgrimage. It is usually introduced as part of a border. The scallop shell, abounding on the shores of the eastern seas, was used by the Pilgrims for cup, spoon, and dish; later it symbolized for them their crusade and was even adopted on their coat armor, an honorable and dignified device.

It was especially appropriate for 'the honoured, ancient Thomas Faunce' as Sewall calls him, whose earthly pilgrimage covered nearly a century and who in his early days had known the real first Pilgrims of Plymouth.

Under this heading of station or circumstance in life would perhaps come those individual symbols, referring to some particular act or event in the life of the person commemorated, like the amputated arm of Mrs. Tripp, Newport, 1780.

IV. RELATING TO THE CHRISTIAN LIFE

A very common symbol used during the whole period is the grape-vine. It is an emblem of Christ, 'I am the true vine and ye are the branches,' but possibly by the New England stonecutters it was considered rather an emblem of the deceased. Mather, speaking of the death of the Reverend Jonathan Mitchell, of Cambridge, says, 'So after the departure of our Mitchell it was feared there would be few more such rich grapes growing in this unthankful wilderness.'

The Church is often called a vineyard, its members the vines, a figure suggested by that verse in Revelation, 'Thrust in the sharp sickle

sickle and gather the clusters of the vine of the earth; for her grapes are fully ripe.'

An early and very good example of the use of a grapevine is on the stone of William Hescy, Wakefield, 1689, made without doubt by 'The Stone Cutter of Boston.'

A late example is a marble gravestone in Bennington, that of Mrs. Sarah Hubbell, 1797, made probably by Roger Booth, who seemed very fond of grapevines and Grecian borders.

When bunches of grapes are combined with ears of corn, they symbolize the blood and body of Christ. This was a combination often made by William Codner, as on the stone of Rebecca Gerrish, King's Chapel, 1743.

Other vines besides the grapevine were employed. Sometimes a bird was placed in the vine, which, they tell us, signifies the soul partaking of celestial food, as on the stone of Pamelia Munro, Lexington, 1770. The dove, which may be the bird on at least some of our gravestones, is typical of Christian constancy and devotion.

A squirrel cracking a nut is said to be a symbol of religious meditation. I have found squirrels on only one gravestone, that of Benjamin Hills, Granary, 1683. These squirrels do not have nuts and perhaps are only a delineation of the gray squirrels which two hundred years ago climbed over the gray stones of the Granary as their chattering progeny do to-day.

This stone of Benjamin Hills belongs to a very interesting group which might be called 'The Urn and Mermaids.' I have found fourteen of this design, of which eleven are in Boston, one in Dorchester, one in West Roxbury, and one in Portsmouth, New Hampshire; this last, however, was erected by a Boston man. There is one other little stone in the Granary, that of the nineteen-weeks-old baby of Mungo Craford, who died in 1688, which has a tiny mermaid rising up behind the inscribed tablet.

Was the representation of mermaids on a gravestone as incongruous as it seems to us, or did the people of that day attach to it some spiritual meaning which we have forgotten? Christ was the son of God, He was also the son of man. He was half God and half man, and the old symbol of this dual nature was the mermaid, half fish and

and half human. Again, in ancient mythology, with which they were exceedingly familiar, the mermaid and the siren were represented often in the same fashion. Sirens were the messengers of Proserpina, whose duty it was to carry the souls of the departed to Hades. So we see why they have wings, and why they are holding the urn containing the ashes, from which the soul is to be separated.

So these interesting Urn and Mermaid stones are a symbol of the close of the Christian life, not of death, nor of the resurrection, but of the last step in our terrestrial journey.

In July, 1693, the Town of Boston was much startled by many deaths from 'the fever of the fleet.' This was brought by Sir Charles Wheeler's fleet, which with two thousand soldiers on board had come to Boston from the West Indies to take part in an attack on Quebec. Two thirds of the soldiers died and many of the inhabitants of the Town. People were 'under much consternation.' On August 6, Sewall writes, 'Capt. Wm. Greenough died about four this morn, buried about nine at night. Three vollies past nine at night.... Brave moonshine.'

And a few days later, on August 17, he records the death of Deacon Jacob Eliot, who according to his gravestone was buried the same day. ''Tis a sudden and very sore Blow to the South Church, a loss hardly repaired. On the Sabbath Mr. Willard being in before me, I did not mind D. Eliot's absence, and wondered I heard not his voice beginning the Ps. and Capt. Frary waited when I should begin it. We shall hardly get another such a sweet singer as we have lost. He was one of the most serviceable men in Boston. One of the best and most respectful friends I had in the world. Lord awaken us. Scarce a man was so universally known as he.'

V. THE FORETELLING OF THE RESURRECTION OF THE BODY AND THE ACTIVITIES OF THE RELEASED SOUL

With the single exception of the almost universal use of the death symbol, some suggestion of the continuance of life after death is the most common.

The beautiful fruit borders of the very earliest times were rarely without pomegranates, understood by all as foretelling the resurrection.

tion. With this the fig was usually combined, denoting prosperity and perhaps happiness in the world to come. Both these symbols, too, brought to the minds of the people of the seventeenth century the 'land of wheat and barley and vines and fig trees and pomegranates' — the promised land. Then, too, they remembered that the pillars of Solomon's temple were carved with pomegranates.

One sculptor, at least, was fond of depicting the last trump, sounded by a young angel with bobbed hair, usually with the words, 'Arise ye Dead' on the label coming forth from his trumpet. There are several of these stones in the old burying-ground in Wakefield; the one here pictured is that of Thomas Nichols who 'exchanged worlds in the month of April 1765.'

Much more common is the trumpet alone — it was all that was needed to bring back the familiar words of the Scripture, 'The trumpet shall sound and the dead be raised incorruptible.'

The rising sun, too, is a very obvious symbol of the resurrection. An early way of depicting it was by the elevated torch, the light streaming up to heaven, while the lowered torch, not so commonly used, indicated the setting sun. Both, however, were typical of life, the former of the sun ascending into a new atmosphere, the latter, of the close of the earthly pilgrimage. The flame arising from the top of an urn has a similar meaning — the soul, separated from the ashes, entering a higher sphere.

Later, when symbolism had to be less occult and more easy to understand, the sun itself was represented and probably always at the break of day. Toward the close of the eighteenth century this was exceedingly common, sometimes engraved with wavy rays, as on the stone of the Glover children, Salem, 1784; at other times the rays are perfectly straight.

The peacock, which I have found but once, became a symbol of the resurrection owing to the fabled incorruptibility of its flesh. It 'was sown in corruption but raised in incorruption.' It was also an emblem of the glories of heaven — Memling in one of his paintings even depicting peacock's feathers in his angel's wings. We are also told that the peacock cries out suddenly when awakening in the night, because it is dreaming that it has lost its beauty, and so typifies the

the soul 'which in the night of this sinful world is constantly fearing to lose the good gifts and graces with which God has endowed it.'

J. N. made a peacock stone, *circa* 1703, for a Quincy blacksmith, John Cleverly.

The world, sun, moon, and stars are often represented, either all together or each one alone. This may have been suggested by the words in Revelation, 'And I saw a new Heaven and a new earth.' It was not this terrestrial sphere where Ann Kilcup, Granary, 1694, had had her share of work and trouble, but the promised new earth, that the carver placed above her peaceful death's-head. And the sun alone undoubtedly typifies the glory of the new life where the righteous shall shine forth as the sun in the Kingdom of their Father.

An interesting stone with much symbolism in regard to the future life is the one made by Henry Christian Geyer for Susanna Jayne, wife of the Marblehead schoolmaster. The hourglass for the passing of time and the cross-bones for mortality are at the top, and just below is the serpent with his tail in his mouth, an emblem of eternity and immortality. Death with his dart is crowned with laurel, denoting victory, and he holds in his two hands the earth and the sun, the new heaven and the new earth. Under his feet are two bats signifying the evil of the world which by Death has been conquered, and in the upper corners are the winged cherubs which redeem the rather gruesome effect of the whole and indicate to us that Death as a conqueror changes us to more happy and more innocent beings.

Possibly most frequently employed of all symbols of the resurrection is that of the redeemed spirit emerging from the tomb or floating through space, making heavenly music on some appropriate instrument. There is a stone in Plymouth, that of Mrs. Betsey Shaw, 1795, where there is represented the brick tomb under a tree, as there are many tombs under trees on Burial Hill. The urn at the side reminds us that the tomb had been occupied, but above it is the redeemed spirit of Betsey just unfolding her wings for its heavenly flight.

Sometimes, as on the stone of Martha Green, Harvard, 1770, we see the reëmbodied person just stepping out of her tomb, in this case with her baby in her arms. This was a favorite design of William Park,

Park, and this stone, in spite of the unfortunate condition of the noses of both the mother and the child, is interesting for its very early delineation of a willow tree which, if carved a hundred years later, we should consider an example of Japanese influence.

The stone erected to the memory of Colonel Jonas Clark, Chelmsford, 1770, has upon it a portrait of the Colonel as he looked when upon earth — a rather typical New England face, shrewd but kindly. Above this are two representations of the arisen Colonel, both resembling the portrait, but scantily clothed in garments he never knew, with wings on his shoulders, a book of heavenly tunes in one embodiment, and a wind instrument held to his lips in the other.

On other stones are represented various denizens of the heavenly world — the future companions or attendants of the departed soul. Nathaniel Phelps has depicted such spirits on the stone of Mrs. Sarah Porter of Hadley, each upholding by one hand her heavenly crown and bearing in the other the legend 'Gloria in excelsis Deo.'

Perhaps the most daring portrayal of the visions of the heavenly life is on the stone of Charles Bardin, Newport, 1773. Here we see the Lord Almighty above the clouds with his arms stretched out to receive the incoming soul — a way perhaps chosen by the sculptor to say, 'Blessed are the pure in heart, for they shall see God.'

THE END

APPENDIX

LIST OF NEW ENGLAND STONECUTTERS
WORKING BEFORE 1800

Those recorded as being paid for gravestones are marked with an asterisk before their names. Those who signed stones with their name or initials are marked with a dagger.

†B. Adams signs stone of Samuel Bent, Milton, 1797
*†George Allen, Rehoboth, d. 1774
†George Allen, Jr., Rehoboth, b. 1742/3
John Anthony Angell, Providence, d. 1756
*Solomon Ashley, Deerfield, 1754–1823
*†Joseph Barber, West Medway, 1731–1812
*Aaron Bliss, Longmeadow, 1730–1810
†Roger Booth, Bennington, Vermont, d. 1849
†Peter Buckland, East Hartford, Connecticut, d. 1816
†John Bull, Newport, Rhode Island, 1734–1808
*Ebenezer Codman paid for stones for Thompson Ingraham, Boston, 1771
*Abraham Codner, Boston, d. 1750
*John Codner, Boston, son of William, d. before 1783
*William Codner, Boston, 1709–1769
*Paul Colburn, Sterling, 1761–1825
†Benjamin Collins, Lebanon, Connecticut, d. 1760
*Zerubbabel Collins, Bennington, Vermont, 1733–1797
Colonel Thomas Dawes, Boston, 1731–1809
*Ebenezer Drake, Windsor, Connecticut, d. 1729
*John Dwight, Shirley, 1740–1816
*John Ely, East Springfield, d. 1735
*Henry Emmes, Boston, d. 1716
*Joshua Emmes, Boston, 1719–1772
*†Nathaniel Emmes, Boston, 1690–1750
*Daniel Farrington, Wrentham, 1733–1807
*Ebenezer Felton, New Salem, d. c. 1741

*Jeremiah

*Jeremiah Fisher, Wrentham. Worked about 1770
*†Samuel Fisher, Wrentham, 1732–1816
*†Samuel Fisher, Jr., Wrentham, 1768–1815
*James Ford paid for stones in 1771
*Hopestill Foster, Dorchester, 1701–1773
*James Foster, Dorchester, 1698–1763
*James Foster, Dorchester, 1732–1771
*Thomas Fosters, Barnstable, paid for stones in 1746
*Robert Fowle, paid for stones in Boston in 1765
*John Gaud, Boston, d. 1693
*Mr. Gauge paid for stones in Boston, 1718
*†Henry Christian Geyer, Boston, d. c. 1793
*†John Just Geyer, Boston, son of Henry Christian Geyer
*Mr. George paid for stones in Boston in 1727
*†James Gilchrist, Boston, 1687–1722
*†William Grant, Boston, 1694–1726
Elias Grice, Boston, d. 1684
Matthew Griswold, Lyme, Connecticut, d. 1698
*Matthew Griswold, Jr., Lyme, Connecticut, 1653–1715
*Isaac Hamlin, Barnstable, Massachusetts, 1742–1810
John Hamlin, Middletown, Connecticut, 1658–1732/3
†Samuel Hartshorn, Franklin, Connecticut, 1725–1784
*Daniel Hastings, Newton, d. 1749
Joshua Hempstead, New London, Connecticut, 1678–1758
*Samuel Hinsdale, Medfield, 1722–1787?
*John Holliman, Salem, 1704–c.1750
*John Holmes, Woodstock, Connecticut, paid for stones in 1725
*John Homer, Boston, 1727–c.1803
*William Homer, Boston, 1770–1822
*Joseph Ingraham paid for stones for Samuel Haley, Boston, 1745
*Joseph Jackson paid for stones for Samuel Allen, Boston, 1770
*Thomas Johnson, Middletown, Connecticut, 1689/90–1761
Andrew Keid, Boston, d. 1802
*Richard Leighton paid for stones for Moses Bradstreet, Rowley,
   1738
*†Caleb Lamson, Charlestown, 1697–1767
                                                        *David

*David Lamson paid for stones in 1798
*John Lamson, Charlestown, 1732–1776
*Joseph Lamson, Charlestown, 1656–1722
*Joseph Lamson, Charlestown, 1730/1–1789
*Joseph Lamson, Charlestown, 1760–1808
*†Nathaniel Lamson, Charlestown, 1693–1755
*John Locke, Deerfield, 1752–1837
Frederick Manning, Windham, Connecticut, 1758–1806
†Josiah Manning, Windham, Connecticut, 1725–1806
†Rockwell Manning, Norwich, Connecticut, 1760–1806
*†John Marble, Bradford, 1764–1844
*Joseph Marble, Bradford, d. 1805
John Marshall, Braintree, 1664–1732
*Levi Maxey, Attleborough, paid for stones in 1798
*Savil Metcalf, Bellingham, d. 1737
*Robert Mulican, Bradford, 1688–1765
*William Mumford, Boston, 1641–1718
*James Nace paid for stones in Stoughton 1782
*Joseph Nash, Hadley, 1664–1740
James New, Wrentham, 1692–1781
*†James New, Wrentham, 1751–1835
John New, Wrentham, 1722
†Hermon Newell, Longmeadow, 1774–1833
†Paul Noyes, Newburyport, 1740/1–1810
William Parham, Jr., Boston, d. 1666
*John Park, Groton, 1731–1793
*John Park, Groton, 1761–1811
*Thomas Park, Groton, 1745–1806
*William Park, Groton, 1705–1788
*William Park, Groton, 1763–1795
*William Park, Harvard, 1779–1854
*Noah Pratt, Abington, d. 1731
†Elijah Phelps, Lanesborough, 1761–1842
*Nathaniel Phelps, Northampton, 1721–1789
Nathaniel Pryce, New London, Connecticut, in 1661
*Hosea Robert paid for stone for Eliakim Stowe of Gramville, 1791
†Jos.

†Jos. Roberts signs stone of Rev. Perlry Howe, Putnam, Connecticut, 1753

†C. Sikes signs stones in 1793

†E. Sikes signs stones in 1793

*Ebenezer Soule, Plympton, 1710/11–1792

*Ebenezer Soule, Plympton, 1737–1817

*†Beza Soule, Plympton, 1750–1835

*William Stancliff, Middletown, Connecticut, paid for stones in 1712

*Ezra Stebbins, Longmeadow, 1760–1819

Henry Stevens, Boston, 1611–1690

John Stevens, Newport, Rhode Island, 1646–1736

*John Stevens, Newport, 1702–1778

*†John Stevens, Newport, son of the second John

George Stevens in Boston in 1791

Jonas Stewart, Dorset, Vermont, in 1790

Isaac Sweetland, Hartford, Connecticut, in 1799

Benjamin Tainter, Newton, 1753–1844

*Isaac Thomson, Middleborough, 1749–1819

Samuel Tingley, South Attleborough, 1689–1765

Samuel Tingley, South Attleborough, 1714–1784

†Samuel Tingley, South Attleborough, 1752–1846

*Jacob Vinal, Scituate, 1719–1764

†John Walden, Windham, Connecticut, d. 1807

*Thomas Welch, Charlestown, 1655–c.1703

William White, Boston, d. 1673

*Joseph Whittemore, Charlestown, d. 1666/7

*James Wilder, Lancaster, 1741–1794

†Ebenezer Winslow, Berleley, d. 1824

†Ebenezer Winslow, Uxbridge, 1772–1841

*Jonathan Worcester, Harvard, 1707–1754

*Moses Worcester, Harvard, d. 1739

*William Young, Worcester, 1711–1795

INDEX

INDEX TO ILLUSTRATIONS
PERSONS AND PLACES

(The places are in Massachusetts unless otherwise indicated. The numbers are those of the pages facing the illustration.)